Detecting shared in social networks algorithmically

By
Himansu Sekhar Pattanayak

Acknowledgement

I would like to thank first and foremost to Almighty, who has been my strength during my whole life.

Then, I would like to express my sincere gratitude to my supervisors, **Prof. (Dr.) Harsh K Verma**, Professor & Head, Computer Center, NIT Jalandhar and **Prof. (Dr.) Amrit Lal Sangal**, Professor & Head, Department of Computer Science and Engineering, NIT Jalandhar for providing me such an interestin topic. Each meeting with my supervisors added invaluable aspects to the implementation and broadened my perspective. They have guided me with their invaluable suggestions, lightened up the way in my darkest times, have always extended me help in challenging times and encouraged me a lot in the academic life. From my supervisors, I have learned to think critically, to select problems, to solve them and to present their solutions. Their drive for the scientific excellence has pushed me to aspire for the same. It was a great pleasure for me to have a chance of working with my supervisors.

This book could not have been written without the encouragement, collaboration and support of my supervisors, Prof. (Dr.) Harsh K Verma and Prof. (Dr.) Amrit Lal Sangal. They encouraged me and scrutinized my work, which helped me a lot to complete my book. I am grateful to the all the faculties and staffs of Department of CSE, NIT Jalandhar for assisting me in many different ways. I am also grateful to my friends and colleague for helping me in completing my work.

I wish to dedicate my work to my supervisors, my parents, my family and my friends for being helpful and very cooperative, who were always there with me and whose blessings gave me courage to make my work success. All of you made it possible for me to reach this last stage of my endeavor. Thank you from the bottom of my heart.

(Himansu Sekhar Pattanayak)

List of Figures

1.1 Karate club network [**Zachary** (1977)] represented as a graph 2
1.2 A network with community structure 5
1.3 Classification of Community Detection Parameters 10
1.4 A network with two communities; the first diagram is non-overlapping and second one has an overlapping community structure with node 21 shared between both communities 11
1.5 Ego network of node 30 colored Indigo 12

3.1 Recall and Precision values for Karate club network 29
3.2 Recall and Precision values for Relaxed Caveman network 29
3.3 Recall and Precision values for Planted Partition network 30
3.4 Recall and Precision values for LFR Benchmark network 30
3.5 Comparing Community metrics for Relaxed caveman graph 35
3.6 Comparing Community metrics for Planted partition graph 35

4.1 Amazon Purchase Network Average Length and Diameter 40
4.2 DBLP Network Average Length and Diameter 40
4.3 Dolphin Network Average Length and Diameter 41
4.4 Karate Club Network Average Length and Diameter 41
4.5 Email Network Average Length and Diameter 42
4.6 Political Network Average Length and Diameter 42
4.7 Youtube Network Average Length and Diameter 43
4.8 Graph Before Execution of Fire Spread Algorithm 55
4.9 Community Detected with Node4 as Seed 57
4.10 Community Detected with Node1 as Seed 57

5.1 Books on American Politics Network 67
5.2 Adjective Noun Network 67
5.3 Dolphin Network 67
5.4 Karate Club Network 67
5.5 Relaxed Caveman Network 68
5.6 Planted-Partition Network 68
5.7 Karate-Club network with k=5.0 70
5.8 Karate-Club network with k=4.5 70
5.9 Karate-Club network with k=4.0 70
5.10 Karate-Club network with k=3.5 70
5.11 Karate-Club network with k=3.0 70
5.12 Karate-Club network with k=2.5 70
5.13 Karate-Club network with k=2.0 71
5.14 The Karate Club network 80
5.15 The Karate Club network with overlapping communities(Nodes 2 and 8 are shared between both communities). 81
5.16 Modularity and Conductance for LFR network with 1000 nodes and Mixing parameter μ varies from 0.1 to 1.0. 83

5.17	Modularity and Conductance LFR network with 5000 nodes and Mixing parameter μ varies from 0.1 to 1.0.	84
6.1	A Erdos-Renyi random graph with 20 nodes and 65 edges.	91
6.2	Difference in APL per degree due to community structure for Relaxed Caveman graph	92
6.3	Difference in average path length per degree due to community structure for Planted Partition graph	93
6.4	Difference in average shortest path length per degree due to number of communities present in the graph	99
6.5	Difference in APL Per Degree due to Size of Communities in Graph	99
6.6	Relationship between difference in APL to ratio of average community degree and average graph degree	101
6.7	Graph with Three Communities	102
6.8	Graph with Two Communities	102
6.9	Graph with one edge reconnected	102
6.10	Graph with two edges reconnected	102
6.11	Original Planted Partition Graph with 40 Nodes	105
6.12	Two-radius Subgraph of Seed Node '10'	106
6.13	Decrease in Membership Values for Nodes of Subgraph g and Seed 10	108
6.14	Community 1	108
6.15	Community 2	108
6.16	Community 3	109
6.17	Community 4	109
6.18	Modularity and Conductance for LFR network with 1000 nodes and Mixing parameter μ varies from 0.1 to 1.0.	119
6.19	Modularity and Conductance LFR network with 5000 nodes and Mixing parameter μ varies from 0.1 to 1.0.	120
6.20	F_Score values for Karate club network	122
6.21	F_Score values for Bottelenose dolphin network	122
6.22	F_Score values for American political book Dolphin network	123
6.23	F_Score values for LFR Benchmark network	123
6.24	A time-variant network, initially had 5 communities, the edges and nodes changed over time and the last network has 4 communities.	124

Conferences

1. Himansu Sekhar Pattanayak, Harsh K Verma, Amrit Lal Sangal, "Community Detection Metrics and Algorithms in Social Networks", IEEE International conference ICSCCC, December 2018.
   10.1109/ICSCCC.2018.8703215

2. Himansu Sekhar Pattanayak, Harsh K Verma, Amrit Lal Sangal, "Relationship between Community Structure and Clustering Coefficient", Springer International conference ICICA, December 2019. **(Scopus Indexed)**
   https://doi.org/10.1007/978-981-15-5566-4_18

List of Tables

2.1	Literature review on network model and community detection algorithm	17
3.1	Real-world network and synthetic networks used for the comparison	32
3.2	Noun-Adjacency Network	32
3.3	Political Book Network	32
3.4	American Football Network	33
3.5	Karate Club Network	33
3.6	Relaxed caveman network with p=0.3	33
3.7	Planted partition network $p_{out} = 0.01$	33
3.8	Planted partition network $p_{out} = 0.05$	34
3.9	LFR benchmark network $\mu = 0.1$	34
3.10	LFR benchmark network $\mu = 0.25$	34
4.1	Average Path Lengths and Diameters of Communities in Percentage	39
4.2	Occurences of edges between node 1 and 2	45
4.3	Path Probability matrix A for Node 24	61
4.4	Residual Probability Matrix R^2	61
4.5	Probability of 2-length Path A^2	61
4.6	Probabilty of 2-length Shotest Paths B^2	62
4.7	Residul Probability Matrix R^3	62
4.8	Probability of 3-length Shortest Path B^3	63
4.9	Residual Probabilty Matrix R^4	63
5.1	Recall and Precision values	68
5.2	Variations in Recall and Precision	69
5.3	Communities with Multiple Resolutions	71
5.4	Specifications of Synthetic Networks	73
5.5	Specifications of Real-World Networks	74
5.6	Modularity and Conductance Values for Synthetic Networks	75
5.7	Modularity and Conductance Values for Synthetic Networks (In continuation of Table 5.6)	76
5.8	Modularity and Conductance Values for Real-World Networks	77
5.9	Modularity and Conductance Values for Real-World Networks (In continuation of Table 5.8)	78
5.10	Modularity and Conductance Values for Real-World Networks (In continuation of Table 5.8)	79
5.11	Compariosn Between CC_GA and FSA Based on Modularity	80
5.12	Predefined Community structure for local community detection	82
5.13	Comparison for local community detection, $F_{measure}$	85
6.1	Average Shortest Path Lengths Predicted using the Proposed Algorithm	92
6.2	Relationship Between Community Structure and Average Shortest Path Length for Relaxed Caveman Graph	94

6.3	Relationship Between Community Structure and Average Shortest Path Length for Planted Partition Graph	95
6.4	Mean Community Size and Average Shortest Path Length Relationship for Relaxed Caveman Graph	96
6.5	Mean Community Size and Average Shortest Path Length Relationship for Planted Partition Graph	97
6.6	Average Shortest Path Lengths	101
6.7	Specifications for Synthetic Networks [**Pattanayak et al.** (2019)]	112
6.8	Specifications for Real-World Networks [**Pattanayak et al.** (2019)]	112
6.9	Modularity and Conductance Scores of Synthetic Networks	113
6.10	Modularity and Conductance Scores of Synthetic Networks (In continution of Table 6.9)	114
6.11	Modularity and Conductance Values for Real-World Networks	115
6.12	Modularity and Conductance Values for Real-World Networks (In continuation of Table 6.11)	116
6.13	Comparison of EFSA with FSA	117
6.14	Comparison of Algorithms for Dynamic Networks	127

Symbols

N		Number of nodes of a network
E		Number of edges of a network
G		Network represented as a graph
g		Subgraph
n		Nodes of subgraph
e		Edges of subgraph
C		Community
$C_c(v)$		Closeness for node v
$d_g(v,t)$		Shortest distnace between node v and t
$C_B(v)$		Betweeness Centrality for node v
σ_{st}		Number of shortest path between nodes s and t
$\sigma_{st}(v)$		Number of shortest path between nodes s and t with v as intermediate
$P(\alpha)$		Proportion of nodes with degree at least α
B_u		Block assigned to node u
q_c		Percolation-threshold
c		Total number of communities
e_{ii}		Number of inside edges of $community_i$
a_i		Number of all the edges with at-least one end of the edge inside $community_i$
$E_{C_i,C_i'}$		Number of edges connecting community C_i to C_i'
$V(C_i)$		Number of edges of community C_i
$P(E)$		Number of potentail edges of network
p_{out}		Probability of edge in planted partition network between nodes belonging to different groups
p_{in}		Probability of edge in planted partition network between nodes belonging to same groups
μ		Mixing coefficient
$D - neighborhood$		Neighborhood wehre maximimum distnce between nodes is $D - hop$.
D		Diamter of community
R		Radius of community

d	Average node degree in the network
P_1	Probability of 1-length path between two nodes in a community
P_2	Probability of 2-length path between two nodes in a community
d_i	Average degree of nodes inside a $community_i$
n_i	Number of nodes in $community_i$
k	Ratio between number nodes and average degree of a graph
T_h	Heat transmission coefficient
$P_{i|j}$	Probability of fire of ith node due to j^{th} neighbor
T_{hj}	Heat transfer coefficient for j^{th} neighbor
$Deg(i)$	Degree of node i
p_{avg}	Average fire propagation probability of the 2-neighborhood subgraph
p_i	Fire propagation probability
n'_i	Expected number of paths with length i
l	Total number of communities of a graph
L	List stores the node degrees of subgraph g
$A[i][j]$	Probability of edge between node$i$ and node$j$
sum_i	Summation of elements in i^{th} row of A
$A^k[i][j]$	Probability of k-length path between node$i$ and node$j$
A^k	Probability of k-length path in the network between each pair of nodes
I	Unit $n \times n$ matrix with each entry set to 1.0
B^k	A $n \times n$ matrix which stores the probability of path between each pair of nodes of g with k being the maximum allowed distance
R_k	Residual probability matrix
dis_{rand}	Average shortest path length of random graph
dis_G	Average shortest path length of graph G
M	Community Membership matrix
$M[i][j]$	Probability of jth neighbor node to be a member of community if i^{th} node is part of the community
$M^k[i][j]$	Probability of jth node to be a member of community if i^{th} node is part of the community when nodes have $k-length$ shortest path between them
M^R	Membership probability matrix with $R-length$ paths
$interval\_long$	Longer interval after which FSA is executed

interval_short	Shorter interval for checking network status
link_threshold	Number links added or deleted after which Local_FSA runs
node_threshold	Number nodes added or deleted after which Local_FSA runs

Abbreviations

SNA	Social Network Analysis
ER	Erdos–Renyi Model
BA Model	Barabasi-Albert Preferential Model
SBM	Stochastic Block Model
LFR	Lancichinetti–Fortunato–Radicchi benchmark network
PSO	Particle Swarm Optimization
LICOD	Leader Driven Community Detection Algorithm
Local-T	LOCAL T Metric based Community Detection
ENBC	Ego Network Based Community Detection Algorithm
CDERS	Community Detection Algorithm based on an Expanding Ring Search
HLCD	Heuristic Local Community Detection Method
LPA	Label Propagation Algorithm
FSA	Fire Spread Community Detection Algorithm
DBLP	Digital Bibliography & Library Project
MULTI_FACTOR	Multiplication Factor
AVG	Average
PROB	Probability
THRES	Threshold
BFS	Breadth-First Sampling
SD	Standard Deviation
GA	Genetic Algorithm
CC_GA	Clustering Coefficient-based Genetic Algorithm
EFSA	Enhanced Fire Spread Community Detection Algorithm
APL	Average Path Length
TFSA	Time-Variant Fire Spread Community Detection Algorithm

Contents

Acknowledgement
List of Figures ii
List of Tables
Symbol iv

Abbreviations v
Chapters x
Abstract
INTRODUCTION xiii
xiv
xvii
xix
xxi

1
1.1 Overview 1
1.2 Properties of Social Network 2
1.3 Common Metrics for Social Networks 3
1.4 Community Detection in Social Networks 4
1.5 Applications of Community Detection 6
1.6 Performance Evaluation Parameters 8
1.7 Overlapping Vs Non-Overlapping Communities 9
1.8 Local Community Detection 9
1.9 Time variant community detection 10
1.10 Methods for Community Detection 12
1.11 Problem Statement 13
1.12 Research Objectives 13
1.13 Significant Contributions 14
1.14 Research Significance 15
1.15 Organization of study 2 15

LITERATURE REVIEW 17
2.1 Overview 17
2.2 Network Models for Real-world Social Networks 17
2.3 Community Detection Algorithms 20
2.4 Local Community Detection Algorithms 22
2.5 Overlapping Community Detection Algorithms 22
2.6 Time Variant Community Detection Algorithms 23
2.7 Research Gaps and Motivation 24

3 PERFORMANCE EVALUATION METRICS AND COMMUNITY DETECTION ALGORITHMS IN SOCIAL NETWORKS 26
- 3.1 Overview 26
- 3.2 Comparison of Community Detection Algorithms based on Precision and Recall 27
- 3.3 Comparison of Community Detection Algorithms 29
- 3.4 Sensitivity of Performance Metrics for Community Detection 33
- 3.5 Chapter Summary 36

4 COMMUNITY DETECTION IN SOCIAL NETWORKS BASED ON FIRE PROPAGATION 37
- 4.1 Outline 37
- 4.2 Localization of Community Detection 38
- 4.3 Probability of Connectivity between any two Nodes inside a Community . . 43
  - 4.3.1 Expressing Probability in terms of Total Nodes 46
  - 4.3.2 Relation Between Community Size and Edge Density 47
- 4.4 Proposed Fire Spread Algorithm 48
  - 4.4.1 Two Radius Neighborhood Subgraph 49
  - 4.4.2 Modeling Fire Spread Algorithm 49
  - 4.4.3 Threshold to Catch Fire 50
  - 4.4.4 Designing the Proposed Algorithm 50
    - 4.4.4.1 Finding Shared Communities 51
    - 4.4.4.2 Distance and Probability Relation 51
    - 4.4.4.3 Fire Propagation Probability for each Node 52
    - 4.4.4.4 Expected Number of Nodes of a Community 52
    - 4.4.4.5 Calculation of Threshold Value 53
  - 4.4.5 Fire Spread Community Detection Algorithm 54
    - 4.4.5.1 Complexity of Fire Spread Algorithm 56
  - 4.4.6 Predicting the Radius of a Community 57
- 4.5 Chapter Summary 62

5 COMPARISON OF FSA WITH OTHER COMMUNITY DETECTION ALGORITHMS 65
- 5.1 Outline 65
- 5.2 Evaluation of Proposed Algorithm in terms of Recall and Precision 66
  - 5.2.1 Datasets 66
  - 5.2.2 Calculation of Recall and Precision 67
  - 5.2.3 Impact of Random Seed Nodes on Recall and Precision 68
- 5.3 Detection of Multiple Resolution Communities with FSA 70
- 5.4 Comparison based on Modularity and Conductance 71
  - 5.4.1 Evaluation of FSA using Synthetic Networks 72
  - 5.4.2 Evaluation of FSA using Real World Networks 72
  - 5.4.3 Comparison of FSA with Genetic Algorithm Based Algorithm . . . 80

	5.5	Comparison with LFR Benchmark Networks	81
	5.6	Comparison for Local Community Detection Algorithms	82
	5.7	Chapter Summary	85

6 EFFECT OF VARYING COMMUNITY STRUCTURE ON NETWORK 87

- 6.1 Outline 87
- 6.2 Algorithm to Find APL of a Random Graph 88
  - 6.2.1 Nodes at 1-Edge Distance from Source 89
  - 6.2.2 Number of Nodes at R-Edge Distance from Source Node . . . 89
- 6.3 Relation Between Community Structure and APL 92
- 6.4 Mean Community Size and APL Relationship 98
  - 6.4.1 Number of Communities and APL 98
  - 6.4.2 Mean Size of Communities and APL 98
  - 6.4.3 Relationship between Average Degree of Community and APL . . . 100
- 6.5 Connectivity Probability of two arbitrary Nodes belonging to a Community 102
  - 6.5.1 Expressing the Probability in terms of number of Community Nodes 103
- 6.6 The Proposed Technique for Community Detection 103
  - 6.6.1 Phase-1: Choosing Arbitrary Seed and Finding R-radius Neighborhood 104
  - 6.6.2 Phase-2: Filtering out Non-Community Nodes from R-radius Subgraph 106
  - 6.6.3 The Algorithm for Community Detection 109
  - 6.6.4 Performance Evaluation of the Proposed Algorithm 110
  - 6.6.5 Comparison with LFR Benchmark Networks 118
  - 6.6.6 Comparison for Local Community Detection Algorithms . . . 121
- 6.7 Adapting FSA to Work with Time Variant Networks 121
- 6.8 Chapter Summary 126

7 CONCLUSION AND FUTURE SCOPE 129

- 7.1 Conclusion 129
- 7.2 Future scope 131

Bibliography 132

Abstract

Social networks are made up of a variety of actors and their interactions. Humans, blogs, photographs, Instagram photographs, news stories, and websites may all be considered as actors. Human communication is growing increasingly reliant on social media. For the past several years, numerous academics and scientists have been interested in the structure and evolution of various real-world networks, as well as their study.

A network's community may be described as a group of nodes that are more tightly connected to one another than the rest of the network's nodes. Clustering (or community structure) is a phenomena that may be seen not just in naturally occurring networks, but also in man-made networks such as the World Wide Web. The goal of community detection is to discover groupings of nodes from a graphical structure that represents a functional unit in some way. Community detection is useful for the applications, such as, detecting suspicious events in telecommunication networks, refactoring the software packages, recommendation systems for online-shopping and entertainment, link prediction, controlling epidemic spreading, detecting terrorist and criminal groups, and controlling information diffusion. However, community detection is a difficult task because there are numerous definitions for community based on various parameters; finding an optimal community based on a scoring function is an NP-hard problem; communities in social networks tend to overlap to varying degrees; and selecting suitable parameters to evaluate detected communities in the absence of ground truth data is a difficult task.

For real-world networks, the early random graph models for social networks were proven to be inefficient. Preferential attachment and community structure models are the most realistic network models. Because of the preferred attachment paradigm, certain nodes operate as hubs, sharing the majority of the linkages. The preferred attachment concept is to responsible for the social network's shrinking width and average path lengths. However, little research has been done on the impact of community organization on network average path length.

Modularity maximization strategies are used in many of the community discovery algorithms. The modularity maximization strategies, on the other hand, are ineffective in recognizing communities of smaller sizes, a phenomenon known as the resolution limit. The time-complexity of the modularity maximization strategies is considerable. Label propagation is the other most effective strategy. In general, label propagation is quicker than modularity maximization. For some networks, however, the variation of communities owing to the order of label propagation is significant. Though the random-walk models are efficient, the time complexity is higher since the random-walks must be longer in order to get better accuracy. Local community detection, where a community is discovered for a specific seed node, is required in many real-world applications. The present community detection techniques at the local level have a relatively high computational cost. Many social networks possess community structures that overlap. For overlapping networks, general community detection techniques that limit each node's membership to only one community are ineffective. Snapshot and evolutionary methods are used to find time-variant communities. The accuracy of snapshot-based techniques is good, but the computing cost is significant. The static community detection techniques must be run repeatedly. Despite the fact that evolutionary techniques have a reasonable processing cost, their accuracy may be limited.

Seven well-known community classification techniques are evaluated using a variety of real-world, simulated, and benchmark networks. Using networks with established community structure, the algorithms are also assessed for precision and recall. For synthetic data sets, all seven algorithms are suitable in terms of recall and precision. For real-world data, recall values aren't extremely high. Label Propagation strategies had poor modularity scores in numerous cases, however Infomap and Multilevel algorithms consistently fared well. The Edge Betweenness and Spinglass algorithms take a long time to run even on small networks.

To compare the techniques for networks with unknown community structure, metrics such as modularity, conductance, coverage, performance, and clustering coefficient are employed. As the community structure was gradually degraded, the modularity, clustering coefficient, performance, and coverage values of synthetic networks decreased. The conductance values increased. Because performance drops only slightly when community structure deteriorates, the performance metric can be said to be unaffected by community structure quality.

The Fire Spread community detection technique is introduced in this research as a novel community detection technique inspired by the fire propagation concept (FSA). When a place catches fire, the surrounding areas are also at risk of being torched. The distance between the source of fire and the present location, as well as the material's combustive threshold, the number of neighbours already in a burning condition, and the heat transmission property of the gap between the source and present location, all play a role in getting burned by fire. The phenomenon of finding a community around a seed node is similar to the phenomenon of fire spreading from a source. The suggested method, dubbed Fire Spread Community Detection Algorithm (FSA), can recognise communities at both the local and network levels. If the algorithm is run throughout the whole network, it can detect all of the communities. If done locally, it can also find a local community based on a seed node. In comparison to the other technique, FSA limits the search for communities to a smaller number of nodes. Because it does not need a node to be a member of more than one community, the proposed method can detect overlapping communities. The algorithm's execution time is proportional to the number of communities in the network.

The average shortest path length of several networks with known community structures is found to be quite short in the majority of the communities. This research lay the groundwork for locating community within a few hops of a seed node. A two-radius neighbourhood network is adequate to search for a local community around a seed node if each node in the community is linked to at least one-third of the nodes within the community. A new probability-based methodology is devised for estimating the radius of the community given a seed node. This is used to automate the calculation of FSA radius recommendations. Furthermore, any of the existing community detection techniques may be used with the radius prediction technique to localize the community detection. The observed communities have high precision and recall values, which were discovered using FSA with certain well-known social networks. FSA functions effectively even in the presence of shared communities. The number of communities in a network does not have to be set by the FSA. When the method is performed locally with different seed nodes, it is observed that it is capable of identifying communities that are quite identical, with little variance. On several synthetic and real-world networks, the proposed Fire Spread algorithm outperformed some of the well-known algorithms for community discovery in terms of conductance and modularity. The suggested technique is also evaluated using the LFR benchmark networks. Other local community detection algorithms that employ networks with defined community structure and are based on the $F_{measure}$ are compared to FSA. For some networks, FSA's performance is greater, whereas for all other networks, it is competitive.

Changing the community structure of the networks reveals the impact of community on network. The study employs both Planted Partition Networks and Relaxed Caveman Networks. The community structure of these synthetic networks is changed, and their effects are investigated. A comprehensive examination of the influence of community formation on network structure, specifically on the network's average shortest path length, is carried out in order to quantify the influence of community structure on the network. Due to preferred attachment and community structures, social networks have smaller diameters and shorter average path lengths between participant nodes, as stated by previous studies. Contrary to popular belief, community structure in social networks causes average shortest route lengths between participating nodes to lengthen. The average shortest path length of a random graph is determined to be shorter than that of a social network with community structure. When compared to a random graph with an equal number of nodes and edges, the difference in average shortest path lengths decreases as the size of individual communities grows. This relationship is used to predict the average size of a community and the number of communities in a network. The following insights are used to improve the performance of the proposed FSA algorithm, which is named "Enhanced Fire Spread Community Detection Algorithm" (EFSA).

Finally, the FSA approach has been adjusted to operate with time-varying networks. After experimentation with real-world and synthetic networks, the proposed methodology is proven to be efficient and equivalent to the results of some of the well-known static community finding strategies.

Chapter 1

INTRODUCTION

1.1 Overview

Social networks play a very crucial role in revolutionizing communication between people and organizations. Due to the impact of social media, human emotions, interactions, and collective behavior are influenced and shaped in a big way. As per the statistics given in [**Center** (2016), **Statista** (2016)], 71% of online adults are using Facebook, 23% are using Twitter, 26% are using Instagram, and 28% are using LinkedIn. In absolute numbers, there are globally 1505 million Facebook users followed by 900 million WhatsApp users, 400 million Instagram users, 316 million Twitter users, and 300 million Skype users. Hence it can be inferred that social media are becoming an integral part of human communication. Structure and evolution of various real-world networks and their analysis has become a principal area of interest for various researchers and scientists for the past few years. However, analyzing the networks by collecting social media data is a challenging task involving high cost and inaccuracy [**Fortunato** (2010)].

Social networks constitute several actors and interactions between them. The actors can be human beings, blogs, photos, Instagram pics, news articles, and websites. Similarly, the interaction between these actors could be the comments on news articles, comments on YouTube videos, the likes on social media posts and tagging in photos.

There are several ways to represent a social network. However, the graph theoretic concepts are quite popular for their use in representation and analysis of the social networks [**Wasserman et al.** (1994)]. The graphs have certain inherent structural properties, which help in better understanding of the interactions between different actors in social networks. A social network can be defined as a set N, denoted as $N = \{n_1, n_2, n_3, ...n_g\}$, consisting of g actors (nodes) and interactions (edges) between those actors. The edges here can be both directional and non-directional For an email network where a sender sends email to a receiver, the edges are directional. On the contrary, a Facebook network is a non-directional network since friendships are mutual.

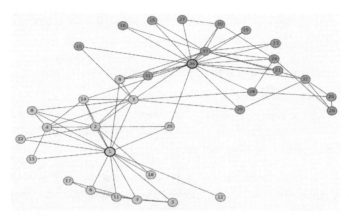

Figure 1.1: Karate club network [**Zachary** (1977)] represented as a graph

1.2 Properties of Social Network

Diameter: Social networks have relatively shorter backbone network consisting of high degree nodes thus decreasing the diameter of the whole network. Diameters are generally refereed doe (i) Network's average shortest path length (ii) Network's longest path length [**Albert et al.** (2011),**Broder et al.** (2011)].

Navigability: Social networks are easily navigable. Any two participant entities in a social network are connected by shorter length path in comparison with other networks [**Kleinberg** (2000b)]. Due to this easy navigability, local information is sufficient to discover the global structure of the network. An arbitrary node in this kind of network can navigate towards any other node relatively at ease by following the high degree nodes.

Clustering Coefficient: Clustering coefficient is defined as the probability of any two nodes connected to a common node directly linking them. In graph-theoretic terms, it is the portion of the triads that form triangles inside the network. The local clustering coefficient for a node v is defined as the ratio between the number of adjacent nodes of v to the number of 2-edge length neighbors of v. The average of local clustering coefficients of all nodes is averaged to calculate the clustering coefficient of the whole network.

Giant Component: As discussed earlier, most of the nodes in the social networks are linked through short paths, resulting in a large component connected and contains most of the nodes. In most cases, any two participants nodes have a path between them.

Time variations: When new friendships or alliances form, the social network expands; when connections become distant or split apart, the network shrinks. [**Ma and**

Chapter 1. Introduction

Muelder (2013)]. Because each node addition or deletion can have an impact on larger-scale patterns like clusters, minor alterations can give insight into the network's growth.

1.3 Common Metrics for Social Networks

There are different metrics used to evaluate a social network or nay real-world networks. Some metrics are to evaluate properties of any specific node and some metrics define the network properties. Social networks are defined as graph $G(V, E)$ with n nodes E edges the common social network metrics are defined as:

Closeness: This metric defined how much an node is directly or indirectly nearer to another [**Sabidussi** (1966)]. It is inverse of the summation of shortest path lengths between a specific node to any other node in the network. Closeness for a network of n nodes is defined as: $Closeness(v) = \frac{1}{\sum_{v' \in V} dist_G(v,v')}$, where shortest path between nodes v and v' is $dist_G(v, v')$ and V is set of edge of G.

Network density: This metrics is a measure of connectedness of a network. It is defined as the ratio of actual edges of the network to maximum possible edges. Network density can take its value between 0.0 to 1.0. A network with network density 1.0 is maximally connected and any network having network density near 1.0 are densely connected. A network with density value near 0.0 is a sparse network. However, this metric is not frequently used for network analysis as the value tends to be higher for smaller networks.

Betweenness: Betweenness for a node [**Brandes** (2001)] is defined as the proportion of the shortest paths that particular node lies over all the shortest paths of the network. The nodes that are at the borders of the clusters tends to have higher betweenness values. The betweenness of an nodes is generally used to measure the importance or influence of a node in the network. The formula for betweenness centrality is defined as: $BC(u) = \sum_{v,v',u(v \neq v' \neq u) \in V} \frac{\sigma_{vv'}(u)}{\sigma_{vv'}}$. where $\sigma_{vv'}$ is total shortest paths between v, v', and $\sigma_{vv'}(u)$ is number of shortest paths which have u as the intermediate node.

Degree distribution: The degree distribution of nodes in a social network can be approximated by the power law of distribution. The power law distribution $P(a) = a^{-b}$ defines the proportion of nodes with their degrees greater than or equal to a. Constant $b > 0$ and genarrly ranges between 2.1 to 2.5 for real-world networks[**Albert and Barabási** (2002)]. The power-law distribution is otherwise known as Zipfian and heavy-tailed degree distributions and is responsible for scale-free behavior of networks.

Centralization: It's computed as the ratio of each node's number of linkages divided by the greatest total of differences possible. The degree to which a network's whole structure is centralized is measured by its closeness. While centralization refers to how structured this connectivity is around certain focal nodes, density refers to the overall amount of connectedness in a network.

1.4 Community Detection in Social Networks

Community in a network can be described as the cluster of nodes which are closely connected to each other than the rest of the nodes of the network [**Girvan and Newman** (2002); **Gog et al.** (2007)]. This densely linked organization of networks, in which society is organized into social groups such as families, villages, and associations [**Feld** (1981); **Granovetter** (1977)], may be attributed to various reasons such as similar characteristics of nodes (or actors) and interdependency between the nodes. The phenomenon of clustering (or community structure) is not only visible in naturally occurring networks, but can also be observed in artificial human-made networks like the World Wide Web, where web pages containing similar topics are connected more densely among themselves [**Flake et al.** (2000)]. In biological networks like metabolic network, tightly connected groups of nodes generally constitute functional units, such as pathways and cycles [**Palla et al.** (2005)]. Similarly, the wireless communication networks such as WSNs and MANETs have clustering properties.

In community detection, the aim is to identify groups of nodes from a graphical structure, that in some way represents a functional unit. For the identification of communities, community scoring functions like modularity [**Newman and Girvan** (2004)] and conductance **Shi and Malik** (2000) are used, based on the idea that groups of nodes have more links between their members than with external nodes.

Community detection often thought to be redundant when various clustering techniques are already available. However, Discovering a community is different than clustering [**Orman et al.** (2013)]. In clustering, clusters are found with high clustering coefficients. However, the clustering coefficient only considers the triads to calculate the value, so it may be possible that a network with high community structure may have very less clustering coefficient if the network does not contain high numbers of triangles. As it can be seen in Figure 1.2, the network has four communities; community1 with nodes [1, 2, 3, 4], community2 with nodes [6, 7, 8, 9], community3 with nodes [10, 11, 12, 13], community4 with nodes [14, 15, 16, 17]. However, as we calculate the clustering coefficient of this network, the value is found to be 0.0. This value of the clustering coefficient suggests there is no community structure in the network, which is untrue. The clustering coefficient is the ratio

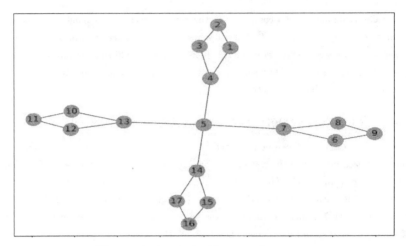

Figure 1.2: A network with community structure

between the number of the triangle in the network to the total number of traids. When triangular structures are not present in a network, the clustering coefficient evaluates zero.

The community structure can be classified into different categories [**Schaub et al.** (2017)]. A network where the nodes belongs to only a single community at a point of time is known as non-overlapping community, On the contrary, in the overlapping community structure a node may belong to several communities at a point of time [**Jebabli et al.** (2015)]. The real-world networks have varying degrees of overlapping. Some real-world networks exhibit dynamic nature. The connectivity between the nodes may changes frequently in subsequent time steps and are known as time-variant networks. Similarly, the community detection is generally classified into two categories, network and local level community directions [**Coscia et al.** (2011)]. The former technique detects all the communities of the network and the later detects only a single community based on a given node.

Finding communities in social networks [**Dhillon et al.** (2007); **Girvan and Newman** (2002)] is a difficult task [**Fortunato and Barthelemy** (2007); **Leskovec et al.** (2009, 2010)] due to several reasons.

- There are numerous definitions stated for community based on different parameters [**Danon et al.** (2005); **Radicchi et al.** (2004)].

- Finding an optimal community based on a scoring function is an NP-hard problem [**Radicchi et al.** (2007)].

- The communities in social networks tend to overlap with each other in varying degrees.

- The search space increases substantially with an increase in the overlapping of communities.

- Selecting suitable parameters to evaluate detected communities in the absence of ground truth data.

- How to deal with the social network that have dynamic structure.

1.5 Applications of Community Detection

- **To detect suspicious events in Telecommunication Networks:** Customers' behaviour can be deduced from their calls and text messages sent over a chat network using group identification [**Pinheiro** (2012)]. To do this, Social Network Analysis can be used on data from a telecommunications company to identify unanticipated customer relationships. This method revealed suspicious links and identified outliers in the populations.

- **Refactoring the Software Packages:** Refactoring is the process of improving the architecture of existing code or making it more simple and elegant without affecting its functionality [**Pan et al.** (2013)]. First, an undirected weighted class dependence network of software is built at the class level, with nodes representing classes and edges representing interactions between classes. The intensity of dependence among connected groups is represented by a weight. The method starts with the assumption that at the outset, each class is a member of a certain group system. Then, at classes that have interconnections or dependencies with other classes that are not defined in the same set, a sequence of class-moving operations are performed.

- **Recommendation Systems:** Customers are recommended the most appropriate items by Recommendation Systems, which predicts their interest [**Zanin et al.** (2008)]. This is an item-based tactic in which the device suggests items to consumers that are identical or identical to items the consumer has already purchased. After that, the products were compared to other products in the network, and the most relevant and preferred products were chosen. The resemblance between two objects is calculated using a cosine-based similarity scale.

- **Link Prediction:** By analyzing vertices and ties attributes in the network, link prediction assesses the likelihood of potential links between vertices. Link prediction is a technique for detecting missed and false connections and predicting their potential life as the network grows [**Tan et al.** (2014)]. The network is partitioned into communities using some partitioning scheme, and the knowledge gleaned from these population constructs is used to forecast links.

- **Epidemic spreading on networks with overlapping community structure:** The role of community structure in the network aided the dissemination of epidemics because community structure requires multiple interactions with individuals. Epidemics are most often distributed amongst overlapping groups whose participants are closely linked [**Salathé and Jones** (2010)]. Immunization approaches aimed at people who bridge populations are more successful than those aimed at individuals who are otherwise closely linked.

- **Detection of Terrorist Groups in Online Social Networks:** With the widespread usage of social networking sites such as Facebook and Twitter, extremist organizations use these networks to disseminate propaganda and recruit new members. Since social media sites have a feature that enables the creator of the website to restrict unauthorized access to their page by setting it to public or private, they are less vulnerable to attack. Terrorists exploit "friend of friend" relationships to manipulate or recruit others who aren't personally related to them. For the identification of such groups, local community detection algorithms are used with a known terrorist or criminal as a seed.

- **Information Diffusion:** The process of Information diffusion is propagation of information from one entity to another through contact. Science and technology, public awareness, sociology, and epidemiology are only few of the disciplines where information is disseminated. An entity (or entities) initiates the process, which is then received by another entity or set of entities. News, social media sites such as Twitter and Facebook, and social relationships are the most common mediums. In the spreading process, the structural locations and features of the entities in a social network play a crucial influence. Because social networks are divided into communities and these communities frequently overlap, information generated within one community can spread to entities in other communities. By detecting and targeting the overlapping entities, this information transmission may be sped up, slowed down, or stopped. In order to discover such overlapping entities (or nodes), community detection is useful. [**Chen et al.** (2009)].

1.6 Performance Evaluation Parameters

The goal of community identification is to identify communities only based on the network topology, without knowing any other information. To characterize the quality of identified communities, many community detection parameters are available. The confidence level of the discovered communities is determined by these parameters. The community detection methods are compared and assessed using these parameters. There are two types of community scoring functions (parameters): those that use ground truth data and those that do not. The ground-truth networks are those in which the nodes' community memberships are known. The community discovery methods may be compared using these networks. There are differences in the parameters for networks with and without ground truth data. The ground-truth network's parameters include precision, recall, F_score, and NMI score. As illustrated in Figure 1.3, the parameters for networks without ground-truth data are separated into four types [**Jebabli et al.** (2018); **Yang and Leskovec** (2015)].

1. based on connectivity inside community
2. based on link to outside of the community
3. based on the combination of inside and outside linkage
4. based on overall network

Parameters based on connectivity inside community:

- Inside density: The edge density of the sub-graph involving community members.
- Inside edges: Total number of edges inside community
- Average degree: Average degree of the nodes inside the community
- Fraction of nodes over median degree: Fraction of total nodes of the community having degree more than the median degree.
- Triangle participation ratio: Fraction of nodes inside community participate in a traid.

Parameters based on link to outside of the community:

- Expansion ratio: Ratio between the links going outside the comuunity to links inside the community.

- Cut ratio: Ration between the edge linking outside to the total edges inside community multiplied by the total number of edges with no end points inside community.

Parameters based on the combination of inside and outside linkage:

- Conductance: The ratio between edges going out to total volume of edges with at least one end inside community.

- Normalized Cut: The conductance is normalized combining the community and complement of the community over the network.

- Maximum out of degree fraction: The maximum fraction edges of any node inside community linking outside.

- Average out of degree fraction: The average fraction of the nodes inside community with edges linking outside to total edges.

Parameters based on overall network:

- Modularity: The difference between number of edge in each community to the expected number edges.

1.7 Overlapping Vs Non-Overlapping Communities

The majority of community detection research assumes that a member node is only a member of one community at any one moment. In a real-world setting, however, a node might belong to many groups at the same time. A member of a sports club, for example, may also be a member of a music group. The inter-community border gets hazy when the nodes of one community overlap with those of another. Shared or overlapping communities are the terms used to describe these types of groups. As a result, non-overlapping communities can be thought of as a subset of overlapping communities with 0% participant overlap. Many real-world problems can be handled more effectively if the network is divided into overlapping groups. The overlap between the communities, on the other hand, adds to the detection process's complexity. The majority of current algorithms are intended for non-overlapping groupings. Another element that complicates the problem is the varied degree of overlapping.

1.8 Local Community Detection

All of the network's partitions are recognised during network level community detection. Local community detection, on the other hand, is the process of finding the densely linked

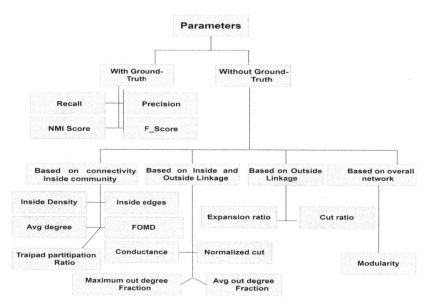

Figure 1.3: Classification of Community Detection Parameters

sections of a seed node's neighbourhood. Node-centric community detection is another name for local community detection. With little information of the network, the goal of this approach is to identify a network community given the seed node as a member. Finding the community structure of a larger network can be expensive, if not impossible, which makes local community identification a viable alternative for analysing a specific node of interest. If information of whether two nodes belong to the same group is required, network-level community detection is not necessary; instead, a local community detection can be performed with any one of the nodes as a seed node and should be verified to determine if the second node is included in the community. We would just need to search a small section of the network for this. It uses less memory and is particularly helpful in dynamic networks with high volatility. Due to privacy policies, most social networks impose various restrictions on the amount of network they provide for public access. In this particular scenario, the local-community detection is helpful.

1.9 Time variant community detection

The communities are functional units that are strongly linked, yet they have fewer connections to the outer nodes. The whole network G is partitioned into l communities as $G = C^1 \cup C^2 \cup C^3 \ldots \cup C^l$, where C^i is the ith community. If $C^i \cap C^j = \phi$, then the communities are non-overlapping, otherwise overlapping. However, in a time-variant network

Chapter 1. *Introduction*

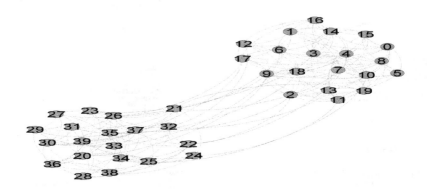

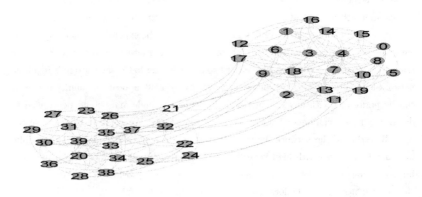

Figure 1.4: A network with two communities; the first diagram is non-overlapping and second one has an overlapping community structure with node 21 shared between both communities

Figure 1.5: Ego network of node 30 colored Indigo

G_t, the network is partitioned as: $G_t = C_t^1 \cup C_t^2 \cup C_t^3 \ldots \ldots \cup C_t^l$ at a time-step t. The network's connection fluctuates dramatically over time, and the community structure undergoes rapid shifts. Over time, the communities may expand or contract. A community's nodes may be added or removed, and some nodes may not be part of the community at all. A community's demise and the formation of new communities are both possible outcomes. It's possible that the communities will combine or separate [**Dakiche et al. (2019)**].

1.10 Methods for Community Detection

There are different strategies for community detection [**Cherifi et al. (2019)**; **Orman et al. (2012)**]. The modularity optimization technique is the most often utilized method of community discovery. The network is partitioned, and the partition's modularity is determined. The division with the highest modularity score is chosen. In addition to maximizing the modularity score, some methods also maximize the conductance score.

The following strategy is based on label propagation. A label is assigned to each node in the network. The nodes send their labels to the neighbouring nodes in each step. A node takes on a new label if the majority of its neighbours do as well. When the labels do not change, the procedure continues and ends. Although it is a simple technique, it is a quick one that is commonly utilized.

A random walk is started from each node in a random walk based model. Each step involves a random probability movement from one node to its neighbouring node. The random walk tends to get stuck inside the densely linked component of the network if the walk is infinitely long. The probability values are used to mimic this random walk. For subgroup identification, the information theory idea is also used in conjunction with the random walk model. The subgrouping is done in such a manner that the number of bits needed to represent the communities is kept to a minimum.

The spreading model, in which the spreading process begins at a node and progressively spreads to adjacent nodes, is also a common paradigm. Each node is chosen as the starting point for the spreading process. For the spreading process, the nodes are tracked. The members of the group share a lot of similarities. The detection is done using the similarity values received from the communities.

1.11 Problem Statement

After comprehensive literature review in Chapter 2 of community detection algorithms and network models, some challenges that remain are: no clarity on efficient community scoring functions, computational cost is high for community detection algorithms, local community detection algorithms have disproportionate time complexities, lack of efficient approaches for time-variant networks.

There exists a requirement to design an efficient community detection algorithm with reasonable time complexity that could work at network and local level, could work for networks having non-overlapping and overlapping community structure, and could be used in case of time-variant social networks. The following research objectives are designed according to the problem statement.

1.12 Research Objectives

- Evaluate and compare the different community detection parameters and assess their efficiency.
- Design a community detection algorithm to detect shared communities in large social networks.
- Evaluate the efficiency of the proposed algorithm using synthetic network and ground-truth network.
- Trace communities over a time period to track their dynamic behaviour and robustness.

1.13 Significant Contributions

The significant contributions of this study are listed below:

1. Seven different well known community detection algorithms are evaluated based on real-world and synthetic networks.

2. The community detection parameters are evaluated by changing the community structures of synthetic networks.

3. Communities of different real-world networks are analyzed and found that most of the communities have average shortest path length less than or equal to three. This results in localizing the community detection.

4. A novel probability-based technique is proposed to predict the expected value of the average shortest path lengths of Erdos-Renyi graphs (random graphs) using only the number of nodes and edges as parameters. The method is faster than conventional Dijkstras algorithm with a negligible percentage of error.

5. An efficient algorithm is proposed to predict the average shortest path length of a community by analyzing the local connectivity patterns around a random seed node before the discovery of local community without the requirement of prior-information.

6. A novel community detection algorithm is proposed based on Fire spread model named as FSA that combines the concept of information flow and probabilistic approaches. The algorithm has low computational cost and does not require any prior-knowledge of the network. The algorithm is suitable of varieties networks. The algorithm is a two-stage algorithm. In the first phase of the algorithms, the local communities are detected by selecting random seed nodes. The second phase is a network level community detection.

7. The FSA algorithm can be used for non-overlapping and overlapping networks.

8. A relationship is established between community structure and average path length of a network by conducting a detailed study. A network with community structure is found to have a longer average path length than a random graph with a similar number of nodes and edges. This relationship is used to estimate the effect of community formation on the structure of the network.

9. The relationships between average size of communities and average path length, number of communities and average path length, and average degree of nodes in network and average degree of nodes inside a community, are established.

10. A new technique is proposed to predict the mean size and number of communities of a network.

11. The proposed FSA is modified to work with the time-variant networks effectively with low computational cost. The method is a hybrid of snapshot based and evolutionary method along with the concept of local communities.

1.14 Research Significance

The research work carried out as a part of the study work, focuses on community detection algorithms and structure of social networks. In this research, the relation between community formation and network structure is investigated and established. The proposed FSA algorithm is capable of working with variety of networks including overlapping and non-overlapping networks and can work at network and local levels. The efficient community detection algorithm helps in finding terrorist and criminal networks from social media data. It is also useful for recommendation systems in online purchasing and online entrainment platforms. The community detection can be effectively used to control the information flow in social networks particularly minimizing the flow of fake news and maximizing the flow of social awareness information. The overlapping community detection can be beneficial in predicting and controlling the spread of epidemic in a society.

1.15 Organization of study

- **Chapter 1**: The Chapter 1 starts with introduction of social networks, social network analyisis, properties of social networks, community detection, performance evaluation parameters. The problem statement, research objective, significant contributions, and significance of the research are also presented in this chapter.

- **Chapter 2**: A comprehensive literature review is done for social network models and community detection algorithms. Research gaps were found, the problem statement and research objectives are proposed accordingly.

- **Chapter 3**: Seven community detection algorithms are compared with respect to community scoring parameters using real-world and synthetic networks. The community scoring parameters are compared by varying the community structure of synthetic networks.

- **Chapter 4**: A two-stage community detection algorithm is proposed based on localization of community search. The algorithm also combines the concepts of fire spread model, information diffusion and probabilistic approaches. The algorithm is named as fire Spread community detection algorithm (FSA) and is capable of handling variety of networks. The average path length of a community is also predicted in this chapter which helps in localization.

- **Chapter 5**: The FSA algorithm is compared with five community detection algorithms based on modularity and conductance and the performance of the algorithm is found to be satisfactory. The algorithm is executed as local community detection and compared with other local community detection methods. FSA is also evaluated using LFR networks by varying the μ values.

- **Chapter 6**: A novel method is proposed to compute the average shortest path length of a random ER network without actually constructing one. The relationship is established between community structure of a network and average path length of a network. A network having community structure found to have higher average path length in comparison with a random network having equal edges and nodes. This finding is used to enhance the performance of FSA algorithm. The algorithm is modified to work with time-variant networks and compared with static community detection algorithms. The proposed method is highly efficient and involves low computational cost compared to the snapshot-based approaches.

Chapter 2

LITERATURE REVIEW

2.1 Overview

Many community detection algorithms and network models have been designed in the past. Only a few of them is discussed in our work. The comprehensive discussions of literature of of the research are is presented in Table 2.1. The literature review is divided into many sections, such as, network modes, community detection algorithms, local community detection algorithm, overlapping community detection, and time variant community detection.

Table 2.1: Literature review on network model and community detection algorithm

Network model	[Erdos P (1959)], [Gilbert (1959)], [Molloy et al. (2011)], [Newman et al. (2002)], [Stauffer and Aharony (2018)], [Milgram (1967)], [Kleinberg (2000a)], [Barabási et al. (2000)], [Eubank et al. (2004)], [Wilson et al. (2009)], [Pósfai et al. (2013)], [Holland et al. (1983)], [Karrer and Newman (2011)], [McSherry (2001)], [Condon and Karp (2001)]
Community detection algorithms	[Newman (2004)], [Newman (2004)], [Newman (2006b)], [Newman (2006a)], [Andersen et al. (2006)], [Blondel et al. (2008)], [Wang et al. (2011)], [Clauset et al. (2004)], [Fortunato and Barthelemy (2007)], [Ronhovde and Nussinov (2009)], [Chen and Li (2015)], [Atzmueller et al. (2016)],[Raghavan et al. (2007)], [Gong et al. (2012)], [Pizzuti and Socievole (2017)], [Shi et al. (2012)], [Zhou et al. (2016)], [Amiri et al. (2013)], [Rahimi et al. (2018)], [Gong et al. (2013)],[Samie and Hamzeh (2017)], [Seshadhri et al. (2012)], [Yang and Leskovec (2015)] [Staudt and Meyerhenke (2015)], [Rosvall and Bergstrom (2008)], [Pons and Latapy (2006)]
Local community detection algorithm	[Yakoubi and Kanawati (2014)], [Fagnan et al. (2014)], [Biswas and Biswas (2015)], [Lim and Datta (2013)],[Tabarzad and Hamzeh (2017)], [Luo et al. (2020)] [Guo et al. (2020)]
Overlapping community detection algorithm	[Lancichinetti et al. (2009)], [Chen et al. (2010)], [Gregory (2010)], [Gopalan and Blei (2013)], [Hébert-Dufresne et al. (2013)], [Kumar et al. (2018)], [Zhao et al. (2016)], [Pei et al. (2014)], [Liu et al. (2018)], [Yang et al. (2015)], [Shen and Ma (2019)]
Time-Variant community detection algorithm	[Hopcroft et al. (2004)], [Asur et al. (2009)], [Greene et al. (2010)] , [Palla et al. (2007)], [Bródka et al. (2013)], [Chakrabarti et al. (2006)], [Lin et al. (2009)], [Zhou et al. (2007)], [Crane and Dempsey (2015)], [Görke et al. (2013)], [Aynaud et al. (2013)], [Lee et al. (2014)], [Zakrzewska and Bader (2015)]

2.2 Network Models for Real-world Social Networks

One of the primary graph models used to describe the social network is the random Erdos–Rényi (ER) graph model [**Erdos P** (1959)]. According to this model, a network having n nodes and m edges, m pairs of edges are generated by pairing among n nodes, randomly and uniformly. An alternate ER model proposed by [**Gilbert** (1959)] fixes equal probability of edges between each pair of nodes. The degree distribution of nodes follows

Binomial distribution. The Configuration model proposed by [**Molloy et al.** (2011)] is an advancement over ER model, where the sequences of node degrees are predefined. The network model proposed by [**Newman et al.** (2002)] suggested the probability p_l that a node in a random graph is connected to any one of the $N-1$ other nodes in the graph is given by the binomial distribution: $p_l = \binom{N-1}{l} \times p^l \times (1-p)^{(N-1-l)} \approx \frac{z^l}{l!} \times (e^{-z})$ where $z = (N-1)p$. A Poisson distribution is the product of this. Once the degree distribution is defined, many of the statistical properties of the modelled networks turn out to be exactly solvable. [**Stauffer and Aharony** (2018)] This research paper introduces a probability q, less than which the network will constitute groups which are separated. Exceeding this Probability of edges between nodes (q) the networks becomes a huge group of nodes. The authors have used a k-dimensional lattice as an example with q being probability of edge. The probability value q_c above which the formation of huge cluster over the network occurs is referred as percolation-threshold.

The small-world principle by [**Milgram** (1967)] explains how considering their often vast scale, most networks have a comparatively shorter shortest path between any two vertices. The "six degrees of separation" principle is the most well-known manifestation of small universes. It was discovered that between most of the persons in the USA had a course of acquaintances with an average length of around six. Most dynamic networks tend to have the small-world property. For example, most actors in Hollywood are separated from each other by 3 co-stars. Similarly, any two chemical compounds are separated by 3 chemical reactions in a cell. [**Kleinberg** (2000a)]Kleinberg raised an interesting point about Milgram's initial small-world experiment that had apparently gone unnoticed by previous researchers. Milgram's experiment demonstrates two essential aspects of social networks: not only can random pairs of individuals in a social network shape short chains of friends, but participants of the network can also create short routes using only local knowledge about their own friends. [**Barabási et al.** (2000)] found an important advancement in modelling and understanding of complex networks using the huge World Wide Web containing documents and links between them: that the degree distribution for most massive and real-world networks greatly distinct from the Poisson distribution defined by a random graph model. Many networks, such as World Wide Web and Internet have power-law tail of their degree spread. Where x is a parametric constant, $p(k) \approx k^{-y}$. Scale-free network was the name given to this network. This distribution differs significantly from poison distribution in that the likelihood of very high degree nodes in poison distribution is very low, while in a real-world network, about 20% of nodes have very high degrees, which is close to power law distributions. It is also mentioned in this article that most actual networks have preferential communication. Links to well-known, common documents with high accessibility are more likely to appear on a newly generated web-page. [**Eubank et al.** (2004)]The authors, by examining the structural properties of big functional networks, confirmed the power-law distributions of node degrees. Most of the real-world networks they examined can be modelled using the power law distribution of links. The relationship graphs originating from Facebook consumer traces have considerably lower amounts of "small-world" properties than their social graph equivalent [**Wilson et al.** (2009)] . This suggests that these graphs have less "supernodes" of exceptionally high degrees, resulting in a substantial increase in average network diameter. [**Pósfai et al.** (2013)] have applied the Barabási-Albert preferential connection technique to graphs with internal vertex arrangement determined by vertices' weights. Weight dynamics are based on the actual vertex degree distribution in this model, and the preferential connection protocol takes all weights and vertices degrees into account. It is shown that a coupled dynamics produces scale-free graphs with exponents that depend on the weight dynamics' parameters.

The stochastic block model [**Holland et al.** (1983)] is used to model networks where the network is arranged as groups (or blocks). Edges are positioned randomly between the nodes. Each node u is assigned to a group B_u in traditional block model. The edge between any two nodes u and v in th network is randomly distributed.The degree heterogeneity was neglected completely in Stochastic block. The nodes are assumed to be having equal node degrees and have equal probability of being connected to other nods by an edge. Real-world networks, on the other hand, typically have a broad degree spread. The stochastic block model cannot be used for many functional real-world networks due its lack of degree heterogeneity. The degree-correlated stochastic block model [**Karrer and Newman** (2011)] modifies the original SBM model and takes degree heterogeneity into consideration. The edge between any two nodes u and v follows Poisson's distribution.The planted partition model [**Condon and Karp** (2001); **McSherry** (2001)], is variant of original SBM model of networks. Here, the network is partitioned into l number if groups. Each group contains k number of members. The probability of an edge between any two nodes belong to the same group is known as intra-group link probability and probability of an edge between nodes belong to separate groups is known as inter-group link probability. For assortative structure of the network, intra-group link probability should be greater than inter-group link probability, otherwise the network is said to have a disassortative structure.The standard planted partition model is modified again to resemble better with the real-world network characteristics by combining it with degree-heterogeneity of nodes. The model is known as degree-corelated planted partition model [**Newman** (2016)]. The LFR benchmark network model combines the SBM model along with the power-law of distribution of links [**Lancichinetti and Fortunato** (2009)]. As opposed to the planted partition model the group size is not fixed in LFR model. The node degrees are not uniform making it suitable to simulate as real-world network. The authors of [**Newman and Park** (2003)] suggested that neighboring nodes of a social networks have similar nodes degrees which is not true for other kinds of networks.

2.3 Community Detection Algorithms

Most of the traditional community detection algorithms are based on modularity score. The work in [**Newman** (2004)] is one of the earliest community detection algorithms. The authors have defined modularity as a quality metric for evaluating the partitions of a network, the partitions are optimized against the modularity value. This method is a greedy method. This method is one of the fastest methods but has limitations in finding communities of smaller sizes. The edge-betweenness algorithm [**Newman** (2004)] uses betweenness values of the edges to partition the network. Edges with higher betweenness are deleted gradually to discover the community structure. In [**Newman** (2006b)], the authors used spectral algorithm based on eigenvalues and eigenvectors with modularity as a scoring function using several public datasets. In spectral partitioning, the eigenvector corresponding to the second smallest eigenvalue of the graph Laplacian matrix is used. A similar kind of work, involving graph laplacian partition is proposed in [**Newman** (2006a)]. Local spectral clustering, mentioned in [**Andersen et al.** (2006)], is an improvement over spectral clustering algorithm, which is based on the concept of finding a cut near a specified seed node. It uses conductance rather than modularity as a scoring function. It also uses Page Rank vector to find and the communities. Another work based on modularity is described in [**Blondel et al.** (2008)], in which the algorithm starts by considering each node as a community and repetitively joins smaller communities to form bigger communities if the joining of the communities results in a gain of modularity score. This method is useful in the detection of hierarchical communities with multiple resolutions. Another work described in [**Wang et al.** (2011)] finds communities based on the hypothesis that 1% of the nodes in social networks are the most active nodes, so it tries to find community kernels from these nodes and adds other nodes to the kernels in the later stages. A similar kind of greedy algorithm described in [**Clauset et al.** (2004)] optimizes modularity by combining different communities to increase modularity score and is efficient in finding hierarchical-community structures. Serious drawbacks of using modularity score as community detection function are illustrated in [**Fortunato and Barthelemy** (2007)]. The use of modularity score restricts the total number of communities of a network to $E^{1/2}$ (E is the number of edges of the network). It fails to find the communities of smaller size, which is known as resolution limit of modularity.

Authors in [**Ronhovde and Nussinov** (2009)] have used an energy model of nodes to find communities. The process starts with putting individual nodes into communities resulting in minimization of the energy levels. The algorithm does this process repetitively until all nodes are placed into their respective communities. Another model based on random-walk and linear-regression is proposed in [**Chen and Li** (2015)], that finds communities by partitioning the graph using maximal belonging coefficient. The work in [**Atzmueller et al.** (2016)] involves the use of descriptive features of the nodes to find interesting structures in a network. Exhaustive search using branch-and-bound is applied to find the best solutions. The algorithm described in [**Raghavan et al.** (2007)], does not need any prior information regarding the network structure, also does not require any optimization of community parameters. During the starting of the algorithm, each participant node is assigned a label and the label are circulated to each neighbouring node. At each step, every node in the network update their label with a label by consulting the neighbouring nodes. The algorithm is a fast algorithm and suitable for large scale networks.

There are some algorithms [**Gong et al.** (2012); **Pizzuti and Socievole** (2017); **Shi et al.** (2012); **Zhou et al.** (2016)], which efficiently use the evolutionary techniques to find communities in a social network. Rather than optimizing a single parameter like modularity, they use multi-objective functions; based on the idea, that a community is a group of nodes having a greater number of internal connectivity than external connectivity. These algorithms try to maximize internal connectivity and minimize external connectivity, in the process of community detection. In each iterative step only Pareto-optimal solutions are stored. Authors of [**Amiri et al.** (2013)] have also applied a multi-objective evolutionary technique to find communities. They have used firefly algorithm to find Pareto-optimal solutions. Some community detection techniques described in [**Gong et al.** (2013); **Rahimi et al.** (2018)] are based on multi-objective functions with particle swarm optimization (PSO). The author in [**Samie and Hamzeh** (2017)] uses a two-phase evolutionary method. In the first phase, global information is used to find community, and in the next stage, local knowledge is used in deep-mining of communities. The proposed algorithm, in [**Seshadhri et al.** (2012)], involves finding Erdos-Renyi (ER) subgraphs to detect communities in a larger network. Work in [**Staudt and Meyerhenke** (2015)] is based on the use of parallel computation on large networks to discover communities. Random-walk is an instrumental technique in finding communities near a seed node by initiating a random-walk from a specified node. More the probability of a node to be travelled in a random-walk, more is the chance of the node being part of the community. In [**Pons and Latapy** (2006)], Community detection is based on random walk model. It is based on the concept that random walks on a graph tend to get trapped into densely connected parts. This algorithm works fine with most of the real-world networks. The authors in [**Yang and Leskovec** (2015)] have used page-rank nibble and random-walk model to find communities locally. The author also classified the community detection parameters into several groups based on internal and external connectivity. The Infomap algorithm [**Rosvall and Bergstrom** (2008)] combines the random-walk model and information coding concept. The method uses probability flow to replicate the information flow in the network. Multiple infinite length random-walks are used to find the probability flow. The partition of the network is based on the compression of descriptions of the modules.

2.4 Local Community Detection Algorithms

Local community detection involves finding out communities around specified seed nodes. The LICOD algorithm [**Yakoubi and Kanawati** (2014)], proposed by Yakoubi and Kanawati, picks leader nodes for community detection. Other member nodes are chosen based on the leader nodes. In the Local-T algorithm [**Fagnan et al.** (2014)], the highest degree nodes are chosen first, and the common triad nodes are joined next in the process. The ENBC algorithm [**Biswas and Biswas** (2015)] also adopts a similar technique as the previous. The nodes' fitness values are computed in the CDERS algorithm [**Lim and Datta** (2013)], proposed by Lim and Datta. Inter and Intra links of the nodes are considered for the process. The local community detection algorithm, HLCD [**Tabarzad and Hamzeh** (2017)], uses a heuristic method by detecting early unstable communities. The unstable communities are then joined. The proposed algorithm in [**Luo et al.** (2020)] selects the nearest neighbour nodes of the given node with greater centrality as part of multi-scale community detection. The local community detection algorithm [**Guo et al.** (2020)] computes the internal forces between nodes for the detection process.

2.5 Overlapping Community Detection Algorithms

The authors in [**Lancichinetti et al.** (2009)] proposed their method which starts from the local level by optimizing the fitness values of each node. Community structures with the highest fitness values are selected. This algorithm can find both hierarchical and overlapping communities. Another similar method for weighted networks is proposed in [**Chen et al.** (2010)]. This algorithm starts at a local level by choosing a node with maximal node strength and adding more nodes to it. It finds communities in the surroundings of a single node. An algorithm to detect overlapping communities based on label propagation is proposed in [**Gregory** (2010)]. This algorithm broadcasts the labels for each node and the nodes agreeing on a label form a community. The algorithm can also be used for bipartite and weighted graphs. Using the Bayesian model, authors in [**Gopalan and Blei**

(2013)] have proposed a community detection technique to find overlapping communities in big networks. This algorithm allows a single node to be a part of multiple communities.[**Hébert-Dufresne et al.** (2013)] have used membership of a node in the network. Membership values greater than 1 signifies that the node is part of multiple communities. Community membership for each node is counted in this work. [**Kumar et al.** (2018)] The authors have used limited information available at the community level to detect overlapping communities. Using simulations, it was suggested that the high-degree nodes are more probable to be neighbors of overlapping nodes. The strategy used in [**Zhao et al.** (2016)] is based on label propagation. However, it is two stage method. During the first stage, the highest degree nodes are chosen to act as seed nodes and neighboring nodes of seed nodes are prevented to act as seed nodes. The process continues until no node is left. The next stage is similar to label propagation; i,e. spreading of labels to adjacent nodes. Each selected seed node has a unique label and is circulated to adjacent nodes. In the end, nodes may be part of more than one community based on the labels of seed nodes.The algorithm proposed in [**Pei et al.** (2014)] calculates the local community gravitation of the nodes. The algorithm detects overlapping communities for a precomputed partition of the network. The authors in [**Liu et al.** (2018)] have used the gravitational method to track the dynamic behaviour of the communities in social networks. The algorithm presented in [**Yang et al.** (2015)] uses 2-hop neighbours of a node to calculate the gravitational force. The algorithm initially starts with higher degree nodes as communities. The authors of [**Shen and Ma** (2019)] have extended the Label propagation algorithm for overlapping community detection using the gravitation method.

2.6 Time Variant Community Detection Algorithms

Some of the real-world social networks are temporal networks. The structure of the network may vary significantly in time line. Primarily, two different approaches are found in the literatures for detection of community structure in a time-variant network; (i) snapshot-based algorithms (ii) evolutionary algorithms. The initial methods to deal with time-variant network is to employ static community detection algorithms to detect communities [**Asur et al.** (2009); **Bródka et al.** (2013); **Greene et al.** (2010); **Hopcroft et al.** (2004); **Palla et al.** (2007)]. The snapshots of the network are taken after a specific time period and the static algorithms are applied to reveal the community structure. The community structures detected at different time-steps are compared. The advantage of this approach is its simplicity to use and reliability in accuracy. However, this approach has a very high computational cost, as the static algorithms are executed many times. In the next approach the computation cost is reduced at the expense of accuracy of community detection. At any times-step, the change in network structure of previous time-steps are considered and minimum change is preferred. There is a trade-off between the accuracy of community detection and smoothness of the discovered structure [**Chakrabarti et al.** (2006); **Crane and Dempsey** (2015); **Görke et al.** (2013); **Lin et al.** (2009); **Zhou et al.** (2007)]. Another disadvantage of this method apart from accuracy is the amount of historical community structure of the network needed to find the subsequent communities. However, the number of previous time-steps required may be restricted, particularly to value one; i, e the just previous time-step. This type of approach is adopted by [**Aynaud et al.** (2013); **Lee et al.** (2014); **Zakrzewska and Bader** (2015)].

2.7 Research Gaps and Motivation

The literature study is divided into two parts; in the first part the study is on network structure of various real-world networks, in the second part the study is on community detection algorithms. The community detections algorithms are also classified as network level community detection algorithms, local level community detection algorithms, shared (overlapping based) community detection algorithms, and time-variant and dynamic community detection algorithms. After studying the literature, the summary of literature review along with the research gaps are presented below.

- There are very few comparisons on the community scoring functions (parameters). Among many community scoring functions, which community function is best suited for community detection is not clear from the literature.

- The suggested network models for social and real-world networks have gone through many changes over the years. The initial random graph models have changed to scale-free network models and community structure in networks is a relatively recent model suggested for real-world networks. The authors have suggested that most realistic network models should be based on Preferential attachment and community structure model. According to the preferential attachment model, a new link added to the network will be preferably added to a node with high degree than to a with low degree. Due to the preferential model of attachment, some of the nodes act as hubs sharing most of the links. Many researchers have attributed the preferential model of attachment for the scale free nature and power law distributions of links for the social networks. The preferential model of attachment is responsible for decrease in diameter and average path lengths of the social network. However, no literature is available which has analyzed how the community structure affects the network structure, to the best of knowledge. We could not found any literature that discusses how the diameter may change depending on the community structure of a network.

- We studied vast number of graph clustering algorithms. Many of these algorithms are variants of modularity maximization techniques. However, the modularity maximization techniques are not efficient in detecting the communities of smaller sizes and this effect is known as resolution limit. The modularity maximization techniques also have high time-complexities. The other most effective technique is based on label propagation. The label propagation technique is generally faster than modularity maximization. However, the variance of communities due to the order of label propagation is high for some networks. Though the random-walk models work reasonably in terms of efficiency, the time complexity is higher, as the random-walks need to be of longer length for better accuracy. There is still a need for efficient community detection algorithm with low time complexity.

- For many real-world applications, the local community detection is needed, where a community is detected for a given seed node. The local level community detection algorithms available in the literature have very high computational cost. The local community detection involves the whole network which is a costly computation for local community. There is a need to design a local level community detection algorithm whose time complexity is proportional to the local community size rather to the network size. The algorithm should be capable of working at network level as well as local level community detection.

- Many social networks have overlapping community structures. General community detection algorithms which restrict the membership of each node to only one community, cannot be used for overlapping networks. There are few overlapping community detection algorithms available, but they are only the extensions of their general community detection algorithms. Initially, the community structure is evaluated as non-overlapping community; overlapping communities are detected in the later stage. Time-variant community detection algorithms are snapshot based and evolutionary based. The snapshot-based approaches have high accuracy, but have high computational cost. The static community detection methods have to be executed many times. Though the evolutionary, approaches have relatively low computational cost, but the accuracy may be very less. In these kinds of techniques, there is a requirement of high memory to store previously detected communities.

Chapter 3
PERFORMANCE EVALUATION METRICS AND COMMUNITY DETECTION ALGORITHMS IN SOCIAL NETWORKS

3.1 Overview

One of the primary areas of social network analysis(SNA) is community detection. Various algorithms are available in the literature for discovery of communities [**Cherifi and Cherifi** (2018); **Orman et al.** (2011)]. Likewise, numerous performance metrics are also available to evaluate the identified communities by the discovery algorithms. In this study, by using synthetic networks, we compare between four well known community metrics, namely; modularity [**Yang and Leskovec** (2015)], conductance [**Yang and Leskovec** (2015)], coverage [**Hagberg et al.** (2008)] and performance [**Hagberg et al.** (2008)]. Seven different community detection algorithms are compared based on above the mentioned parameters. The precision and recall value the algorithms are also compared using real-world and synthetic networks with prior-community membership information.

This chapter is divided into three sections. In the first section, the recall and precision values are used to compare seven well-known community detection algorithms. The algorithms that are evaluated in this work are i) Label Propagation [**Raghavan et al.** (2007)] ii) Multilevel [**Blondel et al.** (2008)] iii) Walktrap [**Pons and Latapy** (2006)] iv) Greedy Modularity [**Newman** (2004)] v) Edge Betweenness [**Newman and Girvan** (2004)] vi) Infomap [**Rosvall and Bergstrom** (2008)] vii) Spinglass [**Reichardt and Bornholdt** (2006)]. The mentioned algorithms are state-of-the-art algorithms and their performances are well verified by the researchers. The algorithms also belong to diversified categories in-terms of their basic technologies such as agglomeration technique, propagation model, random walk model, edge-betweenness, modularity optimization, information theory and probabilistic technique. In the following section, the performance of the algorithms are compared with respect to four community metrics (modularity, conductance, coverage, performance), for which real-world and synthetic networks are used. The data sets used for this work are Karate club network [**Zachary** (1977)], Relaxed Caveman network [**Watts** (2000)] , Planted partition network [**McSherry** (2001)], LFR network [**Lancichinetti and Fortunato** (2009)], Noun- Adjacency network [**Newman** (2006a)], Political book network [**Krebs** (2017)] and American football network [**Evans** (2012)]. Among these networks, Planted partition, Relaxed caveman, LFR networks are synthetic networks and rest are real-world networks. These networks have been used extensively in various researches as benchmark data sets. Moreover, the data sets have predefined community structures which is needed for the comparisons based on precision and recall. The data sets used to evaluate the recall and precision values have pre-exiting memberships. In the last section, the sensitivity of the community parameters are analyzed by varying the community structure of the synthetic networks.

3.2 Comparison of Community Detection Algorithms based on Precision and Recall

To compute the recall and precision values, karate club data set [**Zachary** (1977)], relaxed caveman network [**Watts** (2000)], planted partition network [**McSherry** (2001)], and LFR benchmark network[**Lancichinetti and Fortunato** (2009)] are used. The community membership of the nodes are available prior to the community discovery, for these networks.
. Karate club data set has 34 nodes. It has two communities; each has 17 nodes. The two communities are:
Community1: [0, 1, 2, 3, 4, 5, 6, 7, 9, 10, 11, 12, 13, 16, 17, 19, 21]
Community2: [8, 14, 15, 18, 20, 22, 23, 24, 25, 26, 27, 28, 29, 30, 31, 32, 33]

The relaxed caveman graph has 50 nodes, 5 communities; each community has 10 numbers of nodes. Each community is a clique in relaxed caveman graph and the probability that any two communities are connected (Inter community link probability) is set to 0.5. The pre-existing community memberships of nodes for the five communities are given below:
communities:[[0, 1, 2, 3, 4, 5, 6, 7, 8, 9], [10, 11, 12, 13, 14, 15, 16, 17, 18, 19], [20, 21, 22, 23, 24, 25, 26, 27, 28, 29], [30, 31, 32, 33, 34, 35, 36, 37, 38, 39], [40, 41, 42, 43, 44, 45, 46, 47, 48, 49]]

The planted partition graph has 50 nodes equality distributed across 5 communities.

The linking probability between intra-community nodes is kept at 0.75 whereas the inter-community linking probability of nodes is at kept 0.1. The community membership of nodes is same as given for relaxed caveman graph. The number of nodes of LFR network is 250. The exponent of the power law degree distribution of the network is set to 3.0. The exponent of the power law distribution of community size is set to 1.5. The intra-community link fraction incident on each node is set to 0.1. There are minimum 20 communities with 5 being average degree of the nodes. The community membership of the nodes are predefined. Values of recall along with precision are computed applying the equations in 3.2.1 and 3.2.2.

$$Recall = \frac{\text{Number of community member nodes belonging to detected community}}{\text{Number of nodes of the predefined community}} \quad (3.2.1)$$

$$Precision = \frac{\text{Number of community member nodes belonging to detected community}}{\text{Number of nodes of the detected community}} \quad (3.2.2)$$

Computing of the recall and precision become challenging, if the number of identified communities are different from the predefined communities.. However,a unique approach is adopted to overcome this challenge. In order to calculate the average recall and precision values, the community membership is obtained by applying the community detection algorithm. The assigned communities for every node in the network, by the community discovery algorithm, is compared with the original predefined assignments. The average recall and precision values of all the nodes in the network is reported.

It must be noted an efficient community detection algorithm will have high recall and precision nearer to 1.0. As shown in Figure 3.1, Infomap, Greedy modularity, and Label propagation algorithms perform better, whereas Edge Betweenness and Walktrap perform worse. All these algorithms have high precision, while recall values are not high. Figure 3.2 for relaxed caveman graph, Infomap, and Spinglass algorithms performs best, while Label propagation and Greedy Modularity perform worst. For Figure 3.3, the Label propagation algorithm performs worst, and the other algorithms have very similar recall and precision values. For Figure 3.4, except Label propagation all the algorithms have high precision values and low recall values. In-terms of recall value, Multilevel algorithm has performs reasonably. In all the four data sets, the Infomap algorithm performs consistently. Though recall and precision are perfect measures to evaluate community detection algorithms, the main disadvantage of this approach is that we need to have community membership information of each node of the network.

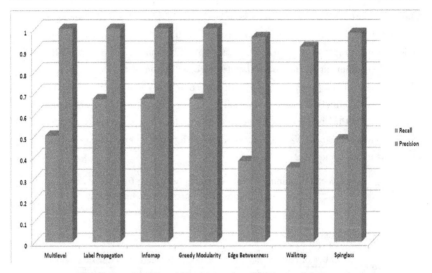

Figure 3.1: Recall and Precision values for Karate club network

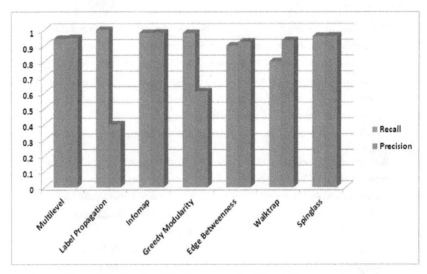

Figure 3.2: Recall and Precision values for Relaxed Caveman network

3.3 Comparison of Community Detection Algorithms

In this section, The above-mentioned seven state of the art community discovery algorithms are compared in-terms of modularity, conductance, coverage, and performance metrics. All

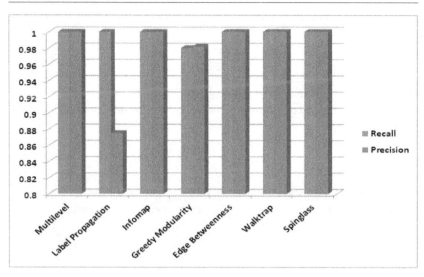

Figure 3.3: Recall and Precision values for Planted Partition network

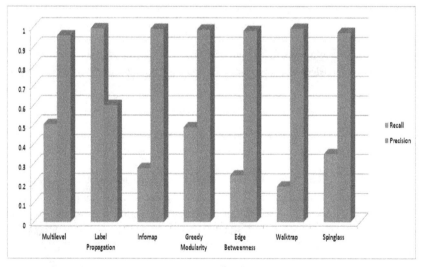

Figure 3.4: Recall and Precision values for LFR Benchmark network

these metrics do not require prior information about community memberships.

Modularity: The modularity is calculated as difference in fraction of inside communities edges to fractions of edges expected.

$$\text{Modularity} = \sum_{i=1}^{c}\left[\frac{e_{ii}}{E} - \left(\frac{a_i}{E}\right)^2\right] \qquad (3.3.1)$$

where E = number of graph edges, c = total detected communities, e_{ii} = number of inside edges of $community_i$, and a_i = number of all the edges with at-least one end of the edge is inside $community_i$.

Conductance:

$$\text{Conductance} = \frac{1}{c} \times \sum_{i=0}^{c}\left[\frac{E_{C_i,C_i'}}{min\{V(C_i)\,V(C_i')\}}\right] \qquad (3.3.2)$$

where c = number of detected communities, $E_{C_i,C_i'}$ = number of edges connecting community C_i to outside, $C_i' = G - C_i$, $V(C_i)$ = number of edges of community C_i.

Coverage:

$$\text{Coverage} = \frac{\sum_{i=0}^{c} E_{C_i}}{E} \qquad (3.3.3)$$

where c = number of detected communities, E = number edges of the network, E_{C_i} = number of edges of community C_i.

Performance:

$$\text{performance} = \frac{\sum_{i=0}^{c} E_{C_i} + \sum_{i=0}^{c} E'_{C_i}}{P(E)} \qquad (3.3.4)$$

where c = number of detected communities, E_{C_i} = number of edges of community C_i, E'_{C_i} = number non-edges of of community connecting outside C_i, $P(E)$ = number of potential edges.

The data sets used for the comparing of the community discovery algorithms are presented in Table 3.1.

As shown in Table 3.2, multilevel, Fastgreedy, and Spinglass algorithms give better results compared to other algorithms. The Label propagation algorithm performs worst. Similar kind of results are produced in Table 3.3 for all the algorithms. The Label propagation algorithm performs exceptionally well in terms of conductance. Multilevel, Infomap, Springlass, and Walktrap algorithms give best results as shown in Table 3.4. In Table 3.5, Label propagation algorithm produces very low modularity value in comparison to other algorithm. All the algorithms perform well for Relaxed caveman network presented in Table 3.6. Similar results are also observed for Planted partition networks presented in Tables 3.7 and 3.8. However, Edge betweenness algorithm performs worst for Table 3.8. In case of LFR benchmark networks, data stored in Tables 3.9 and 3.10, all the performance of all the algorithms are similar, except Label propagation which performs inefficiently

Table 3.1: Real-world network and synthetic networks used for the comparison

Network	Network type	Description
Noun-Adjacency network [**Newman** (2006a)]	Real-world network	Common adjectives and nouns of novel 'David Copperfield'.
Political book networks [**Krebs** (2017)]	Real-world network	Political books purchased by American customers from Amazon.
American football network [**Evans** (2012)]	Real-world network	American football games between 115 college teams.
Karate Club Network [**Zachary** (1977)]	Real-world benchmark network	A college Karate club with 34 members divided in to two groups.
Relaxed caveman network [**Watts** (2000)]	Synthetic network	400 nodes, 20 communities, and inter-community link probability=0.3.
Planted partition network [**McSherry** (2001)]	Synthetic network	400 nodes, 20 communities, and p_{out}=0.01.
Planted partition network [**McSherry** (2001)]	Synthetic network	400 nodes, 20 communities, and p_{out}=0.05.
LFR network [**Lancichinetti and Fortunato** (2009)]	Synthetic benchmark network	300 nodes, μ=0.1
LFR network [**Lancichinetti and Fortunato** (2009)]	Synthetic benchmark network	300 nodes, μ=0.25

Table 3.2: Noun-Adjacency Network

Algorithm	Modularity	Conductance	Coverage	Performance
Multilevel	0.289	0.544	0.466	0.841
Label Propagation	0.017	0.950	0.995	0.068
Infomap	0.009	0.5	0.990	0.12
Fastgreedy	0.295	0.532	0.482	0.833
Edge Betweenness	0.08	0.936	0.278	0.921
Walktrap	0.216	0.816	0.497	0.846
Spinglass	0.311	0.538	0.464	0.857

Table 3.3: Political Book Network

Algorithm	Modularity	Conductance	Coverage	Performance
Multilevel	0.52	0.205	0.853	0.76
Label Propagation	0.442	0.0538	0.955	0.554
Infomap	0.523	0.28	0.855	0.777
Fastgreedy	0.502	0.255	0.918	0.689
Edge Betweenness	0.517	0.252	0.905	0.717
Walktrap	0.507	0.207	0.914	0.698
Spinglass	0.526	0.272	0.816	0.809

in Table 3.10. All these algorithms have high level of convergence for synthetic network. However, the performances vary with real-world networks. Though a fast algorithm, Label propagation performs inefficiently in some cases. Spinglass and Edge betweenness algorithms take huge time to implement even for medium and smaller networks. Moreover, these two algorithms can only work for connected networks.

Table 3.4: American Football Network

Algorithm	Modularity	Conductance	Coverage	Performance
Multilevel	0.605	0.294	0.708	0.942
Label Propagation	0.58	0.367	0.663	0.957
Infomap	0.6	0.337	0.69	0.955
Fastgreedy	0.55	0.278	0.731	0.868
Edge Betweenness	0.6	0.308	0.7	0.937
Walktrap	0.603	0.294	0.705	0.943
Spinglass	0.601	0.298	0.705	0.942

Table 3.5: Karate Club Network

Algorithm	Modularity	Conductance	Coverage	Performance
Multilevel	0.419	0.288	0.731	0.804
Label Propagation	0.133	0.25	0.949	0.383
Infomap	0.402	0.201	0.821	0.711
Fastgreedy	0.381	0.281	0.757	0.715
Edge Betweenness	0.401	0.454	0.692	0.811
Walktrap	0.353	0.408	0.59	0.831
Spinglass	0.42	0.288	0.731	0.804

Table 3.6: Relaxed caveman network with p=0.3

Algorithm	Modularity	Conductance	Coverage	Performance
Multilevel	0.697	0.2528	0.747	0.976
Label Propagation	0.687	0.258	0.742	0.97
Infomap	0.687	0.263	0.737	0.975
Fastgreedy	0.638	0.243	0.757	0.907
Edge Betweenness	0.687	0.263	0.737	0.975
Walktrap	0.69	0.257	0.743	0.976
Spinglass	0.68	0.271	0.729	0.974

Table 3.7: Planted partition network $p_{out} = 0.01$

Algorithm	Modularity	Conductance	Coverage	Performance
Multilevel	0.727	0.217	0.782	0.972
Label Propagation	0.726	0.22	0.781	0.971
Infomap	0.741	0.21	0.79	0.9777
Fastgreedy	0.678	0.234	0.769	0.934
Edge Betweenness	0.733	0.217	0.783	0.977
Walktrap	0.731	0.219	0.781	0.976
Spinglass	0.72	0.266	0.769	0.976

3.4 Sensitivity of Performance Metrics for Community Detection

In this section, four community metrics, modularity, conductance, coverage, and performance, along with clustering coefficient is compared by varying the community structure.

Table 3.8: Planted partition network $p_{out} = 0.05$

Algorithm	Modularity	Conductance	Coverage	Performance
Multilevel	0.353	0.582	0.423	0.92
Label Propagation	0.347	0.582	0.434	0.906
Infomap	0.358	0.592	0.408	0.937
Fastgreedy	0.26	0.532	0.518	0.749
Edge Betweenness	0.176	0.978	0.211	0.923
Walktrap	0.361	0.589	0.412	0.938
Spinglass	0.356	0.613	0.405	0.938

Table 3.9: LFR benchmark network $\mu = 0.1$

Algorithm	Modularity	Conductance	Coverage	Performance
Multilevel	0.8	0.073	0.928	0.897
Label Propagation	0.78	0.137	0.902	0.9056
Infomap	0.798	0.093	0.925	0.899
Fastgreedy	0.798	0.074	0.927	0.896
Edge Betweenness	0.8	0.073	0.928	0.897
Walktrap	0.798	0.093	0.925	0.899
Spinglass	0.792	0.33	0.919	0.899

Table 3.10: LFR benchmark network $\mu = 0.25$

Algorithm	Modularity	Conductance	Coverage	Performance
Multilevel	0.516	0.363	0.645	0.883
Label Propagation	0.23	0.317	0.875	0.333
Infomap	0.511	0.493	0.606	0.926
Fastgreedy	0.494	0.367	0.658	0.854
Edge Betweenness	0.514	0.36	0.65	0.879
Walktrap	0.504	0.415	0.625	0.895
Spinglass	0.538	0.34	0.666	0.885

Though clustering coefficient [Saramäki et al. (2007)] is analyzed along with four community metrics, it can not be used as community metric as clustering coefficient is computed for the whole network and it is not used for the partitions of a network. Synthetic networks, relaxed caveman graph and planted partition graphs, are used for this experiment. Each of the networks contains 400 nodes equally distributed across 20 communities. The inter-community link probability of the relaxed caveman graph is varied from 0.05 to 1.0 (20 networks). The inter-community nodes' edge probability for planted partition graph is varied from 0.002 to 0.04 (20 networks). As the inter-community link probability for the relaxed caveman graph and inter community nodes' edge probability for planted partition graph is increased gradually, the community structure of the graphs get distorted.

The modularity, coverage, clustering coefficient values decrease and approaches zero as the community structures is distorted gradually for Relaxed caveman network, shown in

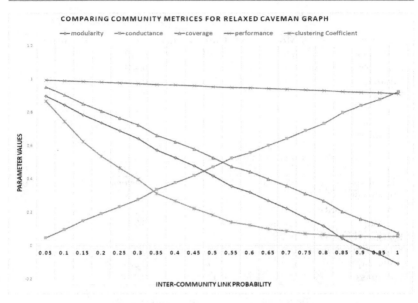

Figure 3.5: Comparing Community metrics for Relaxed caveman graph

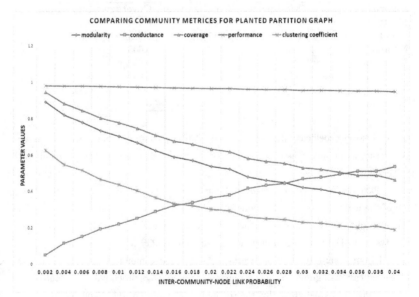

Figure 3.6: Comparing Community metrics for Planted partition graph

Figure 3.5. The modularity values are negative for some networks. The performance value decreases gradually, but not considerably. The conductance increases gradually from 0.0 to 1.0. Similar, results can be seen for Planted partition network, in Figure 3.6. The modularity, coverage, clustering coefficient values decrease gradually from 1.0 to 0.0. There are marginal decreases in performance values. The conductance increases from 0.0 to 1.0, gradually. From this experiment, we can conclude that all these metrics are sensitive to community structure of the graph except performance. Though clustering coefficient is sensitive to community structure, it cannot be used to evaluate partitions.

3.5 Chapter Summary

We conclude, by the experiments presented above, that all of the seven detection algorithms perform well with synthetic data sets showing high values of recall and precision, however the algorithms are not as good for the real-world networks. Among all the algorithms, Infomap and Multilevel algorithms produced consistently good results for both recall and precision.

In the second section of the result,it is found that, all seven state-of-the-art algorithms produce similar results barring few cases. Infomap and Multilevel algorithms perform consistently, while Label Propagation algorithms produced very low modularity values in some cases. Execution time for Edge Betweeness algorithm and Spinglass algorithms are high even for smaller size networks. These two algorithms can work only with connected networks. Therefore, in the subsequent studies, these two algorithms will not be used for comparisons.

In the last section, synthetic network are used for the experiment. Community structures of theses networks are destroyed gradually. It is found that, the modularity, clustering coefficient, and coverage values decreased, whereas conductance values increased. As the performance decrease marginally with decreasing community structure, we conclude that the performance metric is not sensitive to the quality of community structure.

Chapter 4

COMMUNITY DETECTION IN SOCIAL NETWORKS BASED ON FIRE PROPAGATION

4.1 Outline

Community detection is one of the key problem areas in social network analysis. It is classified as an NP-hard problem. Although a lot of good approximate algorithms are available for finding clusters in social networks, all those algorithms have serious drawbacks. They have high time complexities and are inefficient in finding shared communities, a phenomenon common in real-world social networks. The state of the art algorithms,such as, Label propagation [**Raghavan et al.** (2007)], Infomap [**Rosvall and Bergstrom** (2008)], Multilevel [**Blondel et al.** (2008)], and Walktrap [**Pons and Latapy** (2006)] are inefficient in-terms of finding local communities. Though,there are some local community detection algorithms present in the literature, they have to scan the entire network to detect a local community.

In this work a novel community detection algorithm is proposed, that is inspired by the fire propagation model, and is named as Fire Spread community detection algorithm (FSA). When a place catches fire, its nearby places are also at risk of getting burned by it. Getting burned by fire depends on several factors, such as distance from the source of fire, the combustive threshold of the material, number of neighbors already in burning state and heat transmission property of the gap between source and current place. Finding a community near a seed node resembles the phenomena of fire propagation originating from a source. The proposed algorithm, named as, Fire Spread Community detection algorithm (FSA) is capable of performing local and network level community detection as well. The algorithm can detect all the communities if executed over the whole network. It can also find a local community based on a seed node, if executed at a local level. FSA localizes the search of communities to fewer nodes in comparison with the other algorithm. The proposed algorithm is also capable of finding overlapping communities as it does not restrict a node to be part of more than one communities. The running time of the algorithm is proportional to the number of communities present in the network.

In the first section of this chapter, various networks with known community structures are analyzed and it is found that most of the communities have very short average shortest path length. This analysis laid foundation to localize the community detection within few hop distance from a seed node. In the next section, a theoretical analysis on the probability of connectivity between any two nodes inside a network is presented. In the last section of this chapter, a novel fire spread community detection algorithm is proposed based on the findings of the previous two sections.

4.2 Localization of Community Detection

Most of the overlapping community detection algorithms work at the network level. Utilizing parallel computation becomes difficult without affecting the results. In this section, we demonstrate the use of localized community detection based on the diameter of the communities. The maximum eccentricity of any node in the graph is known as the diameter of the graph. The eccentricity of a node is the maximum of its shortest distances to any other nodes. To calculate the graph's diameter, find all pair shortest paths, and the maximum value of the shortest path is the graph's diameter.

Various Social networks, such as, Amazon Purchase network [**Yang and Leskovec** (2015)], DBLP network [**Yang and Leskovec** (2015)], Dolphin network [**Lusseau et al.** (2003)], Karate Club network [**Zachary** (1977)], Email network [**Yang and Leskovec** (2015)], American Political Book network [**Krebs** (2017)], and YouTube network [**Yang and Leskovec** (2015)] are analyzed by computing the Diameters and average path lengths

Chapter 4. Community Detection in Social Networks Based on Fire Propagation

Table 4.1: Average Path Lengths and Diameters of Communities in Percentage

Networks	Cumulative Percentage of Average Path Length		Cumulative Percentage of Diameter Value	
Amazon	Less or equal to 2 84.86%	Less or equal to 3 96.82%	Less or equal to 5 93.0%	Less or equal to 6 96.4%
DBLP	Less or equal to 2 89.3%	Less or equal to 3 98.04%	Less or equal to 4 94.64%	Less or equal to 5 97.06%
Dolphin	Less or equal to 2 Nil	Less or equal to 3 100%	Less or equal to 4 100%	Less or equal to 5 Nil
Karate	Less or equal to 2 100%	Less or equal to 3 Nil	Less or equal to 3 100%	Less or equal to 4 Nil
Email	Less or equal to 2 85.71%	Less or equal to 3 97.62%	Less or equal to 4 92.86%	Less or equal to 5 97.62%
Book	Less or equal to 2 100%	Less or equal to 3 Nil	Less or equal to 4 100%	Less or equal to 5 Nil
Youtube	Less or equal to 2 81.44%	Less or equal to 3 97.58%	Less or equal to 4 94.18%	Less or equal to 5 97.02%

of the communities contained inside the social networks. The community memberships of all the nodes of these networks were previously known. Figures 4.1-4.7 show the average path lengths and diameters of the networks mentioned above in histograms and line plots. In Histogram analysis, the percentages of communities with different average path lengths and diameters are presented. In line-plots, the cumulative percentage of communities with different average path lengths and diameters are presented. These networks belong to diverse domains and vary in their sizes. Some networks, e.g., YouTube, Amazon, and DBLP, are larger networks, whereas Karate, Dolphin, and Political Book networks, are smaller networks.

For the amazon network, 85% of communities have average path length less than Two, and 97% of communities have path length less than Three, 93% of communities have a diameter less than Five, and 97% have a diameter less than Six. In the DBLP network, 90% of communities have an average path length of less than Two, and 98% of communities have an average path length of less than Three. In the Dolphin network, all the communities have less than Three average path length and less than Four diameter. In the Karate network, all the communities have less than or equal to Two as average path length and Three as diameter. For the email network, 86% of communities have path length less than or equal to Two, and 98% of communities have path length less than or equal to Three; 97% have a diameter less than Four, and 98% have a diameter less than Five. In Political book network, all the communities have path length less than or equal to Two and diameter less than equal to Four. For the YouTube network, 82% of communities have path length less than Two, and 98% of communities have path length less than Three; 95% of communities have a diameter less than or equal to Five, and 97% of communities have a diameter less than or equal to Six.

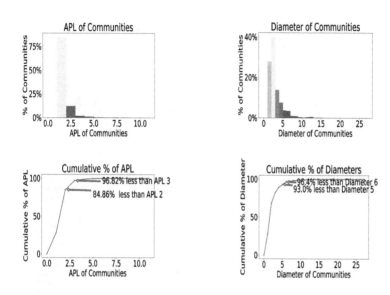

Figure 4.1: Amazon Purchase Network Average Length and Diameter

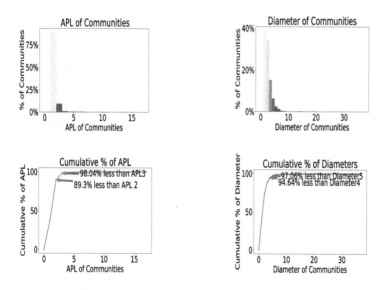

Figure 4.2: DBLP Network Average Length and Diameter

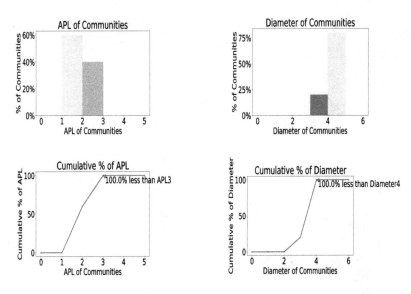

Figure 4.3: Dolphin Network Average Length and Diameter

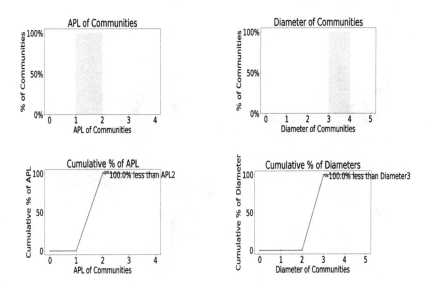

Figure 4.4: Karate Club Network Average Length and Diameter

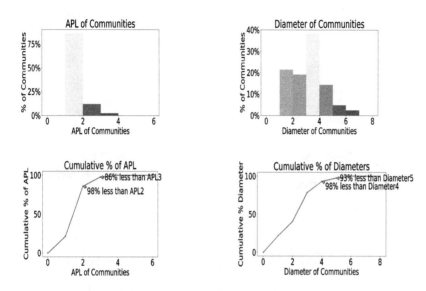

Figure 4.5: Email Network Average Length and Diameter

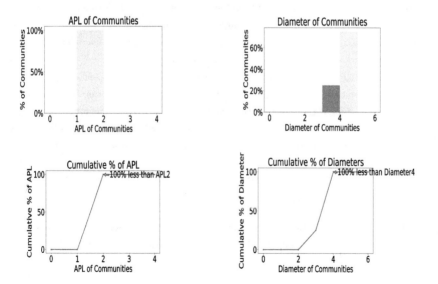

Figure 4.6: Political Network Average Length and Diameter

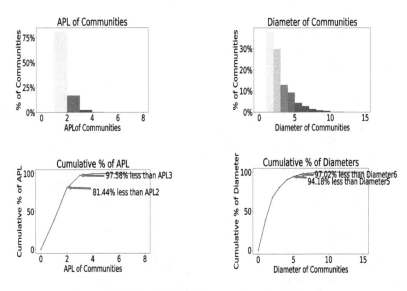

Figure 4.7: Youtube Network Average Length and Diameter

As shown in Table 4.1, most communities have an average path length less than or equal to *Three* for larger networks and less than or equal to *Two* for smaller networks. Similarly, most of the communities in larger network diameters have diameters less than or equal to *Six*, and in smaller networks, it is less than or equal to *Four*. Therefore, the searching of communities can be localized around a random seed node if we consider the D-neighborhood to search for the member nodes. The meaning of D-neighborhood here is the nodes with at most D-hop distant from seed. However, selecting the appropriate values of D is quite determinant for the quality of the discovered communities. Localizing the search in D-neighborhood of a random seed node may help parallelized the process as searching for one community will not affect the searching of another community.

4.3 Probability of Connectivity between any two Nodes inside a Community

Let G be a graph, g is a two-radius neighborhood subgraph with seed s. C is a community inside g with n number of nodes and d being average node degree. Value of d is given by equation 4.3.1:

$$d = \frac{1}{\sum_{\forall i \in g} G.degree(i)} \qquad (4.3.1)$$

Let $n1$ and $n2$ be two nodes inside community C.

$$\text{Probability that both the nodes are connected inside } C\ (P) =$$
$$\text{Probability that nodes are connected by } 1 - \text{edge distance } (P_1) + \qquad (4.3.2)$$
$$\text{Probability that nodes are connected by } 2 - \text{edge distance } (P_2)$$

Let C be a community with n number of nodes, $d1$ is the degree of node $n1$ and $d2$ is the degree of node $n2$. The value of P_1 is given by equation 4.3.3.

$$P_1 = \frac{\binom{n-2}{d1-1} * \binom{n-2}{d2-1}}{\binom{n-2}{d1-1} * \binom{n-2}{d2-1} + \binom{n-2}{d1} * \binom{n-2}{d2}} \qquad (4.3.3)$$

The above equation represents ratio between number of occurrences with direct-edge connectivity of $n1$ and $n2$ to total number of possible occurrences. If it is assumed that node $n1$ and $n2$ are already connected by an edge(self-loop is not considered), then available number of nodes to be connected will be $n-2$(for both $n1$ and $n2$). Since these two nodes are directly linked to each other by an edge, $n1$ and $n2$ can now connect to $d1 - 1$ and $d2 - 1$ number of nodes (by direct edges). Therefore, the total number of occurrences of the direct-edge connectivity is calculated as $\binom{n-2}{d1-1} * \binom{n-2}{d2-1}$. If it is assumed that, $n1$ and $n2$ are not connected directly by an edge, then the occurrences of not connected directly = $\binom{n-2}{d1} * \binom{n-2}{d2}$, since we have $n-2$ number of nodes available for the connections with both $n1$ and $n2$. The total number of occurrences = number of occurrences where $n1$ and $n2$ are connected directly by an edge + number of occurrence where $n1$ and $n2$ are not connected directly by an edge.

The value of P_1 after replacing $d1$ and $d2$ with d in equation 4.3.3 is given as below:

$$P_1 = \frac{\binom{n-2}{d-1}^2}{\binom{n-2}{d-1}^2 + \binom{n-2}{d}^2} \qquad (4.3.4)$$

$$\Rightarrow P_1 = \frac{\frac{(n-2)!^2}{(d-1)!^2 * (n-d-1)!^2}}{\frac{(n-2)!^2}{(d-1)!^2 * (n-d-1)!^2} + \frac{(n-2)!^2}{d!^2 * (n-d-2)!^2}}$$

Simplifying the above equation, the value of P_1 is given by equation 4.3.5.

$$P_1 = \frac{d^2}{d^2 + (n-d-1)^2} \qquad (4.3.5)$$

Let G be a graph with a set of nodes $\{1, 2, 3, 4, 5, 6\}$, having average node degree 2.0. The possibilities of direct-edges between node 1 and 2 are shown in the following

Chapter 4. *Community Detection in Social Networks Based on Fire Propagation*   45

Table 4.2: Occurences of edges between node 1 and 2

Occurrences	Possible Edges for Node 1	Possible Edges for Node 2
Node 1 and 2 connected by an edge	(1-2), (1-3) (1-2), (1-4) (1-2), (1-5) (1-2), (1-6)	(2-1), (2-3) (2-1), (2-4) (2-1), (2-5) (2-1), (2-6)
Node 1 and 2 not connected by an edge	(1-3), (1-4) (1-3), (1-5) (1-3), (1-6) (1-4), (1-5) (1-4), (1-6) (1-5), (1-5)	(2-3), (2-4) (2-3), (2-5) (2-3), (2-6) (2-4), (2-5) (2-4), (2-6) (2-5), (2-6)

table. Total number of possible edges between node 1 and 2 = $\binom{4}{1} * \binom{4}{1} = 4 * 4 = 16$, as shown in Table 4.2. Similarly, the number of occurrences when node 1 and 2 are not connected directly, is calculated as $\binom{4}{2} * \binom{4}{2} = 6 * 6 = 36$. Therefore, the probability that node 1 and 2 are directly connected $= \frac{16}{16+36} \approx 0.31$.

Next requirement is to calculate the value of P_2. Let C be a community which has n nodes and d be its average node degree. $n1$ and $n2$ are two nodes belonging to a community C, and they are not connected directly. If it is assumed that these two nodes are connected though an intermediate node $n3$; the node $n3$ can be any of the $n-2$ number of nodes except $n1$ and $n2$. Now, node $n1$ is connected to $n3$ and node $n2$ is also connected to $n3$. The probability of $n1$ connected to $n3$ and $n2$ connected to $n3$ are denoted as q_1 and q_2, respectively. Therefore, P_2 can be written as:

$$P_2 = q_1 * q_2 * (n-2) \qquad (4.3.6)$$

In the above equation $n-2$ is multiplied, since there are $n-2$ possibilities of intermediate nodes that can act as $n3$.

Next requirement is to calculate the value of q_1. As already assumed, $n1$ and $n2$ are not connected directly. Since $n1$ and $n3$ are connected by an edge, $n1$ can now connect from $n-3$ available nodes (except $n1$, $n2$ and $n3$) and $n3$ can connect from $n-2$ available nodes (except $n1$ and $n3$). As, both these nodes are already connected by an edge, they can now be linked to $d-1$ number of nodes through direct edges.

$$\begin{aligned} D_1 &= number\ of\ occurrences\ when\ n1\ and\ n3\ are\ connected \\ &= \binom{n-3}{d-1} * \binom{n-2}{d-1} \\ &= \frac{(n-3)!}{(d-1)! * (n-d-2)!} * \frac{(n-2)!}{(d-1)! * (n-d-1)!} \end{aligned}$$

$$\Rightarrow D_1 = \frac{(n-3)!^2 * (n-2)}{(d-1)!^2 * (n-d-2)!^2 * (n-d-1)} \tag{4.3.7}$$

Let D_2 be the number of occurrences when $n1$ and $n3$ are not connected. In this case, $n1$ and $n2$ have $n-3$ and $n-2$ available nodes to connect. Both the nodes can now select d number of nodes to link.

$$D_2 = Probability\ n1\ and\ n3\ are\ not\ connected$$

$$= \binom{n-3}{d} * \binom{n-2}{d}$$

$$= \frac{(n-3)!}{d! * (n-d-3)!} * \frac{(n-2)!}{d! * (n-d-2)!}$$

$$\Rightarrow D_2 = \frac{(n-3)!^2 * (n-2)}{d!^2 * (n-d-3)!^2 * (n-d-2)} \tag{4.3.8}$$

$$q_1 = \frac{D_1}{D_1 + D_2}$$

By simplifying the above expression,

$$q_1 = q_2 = \frac{d^2}{d^2 + (n-d-1) * (n-d-2)} \tag{4.3.9}$$

The values for q_1 and q_2 are same and replacing their values in equation 4.3.6:

$$P_2 = \left(\frac{d^2}{d^2 + (n-d-1) * (n-d-2)}\right)^2 * (n-2) \tag{4.3.10}$$

Similarly, if three-radius neighborhood graph is considered, then the probability that any two nodes of the community are connected by 3-length path, denoted as P_3, can be calculated as (similar to calculations of P_2):

$$P_3 = \left(\frac{d^2}{d^2 + (n-d-2) * (n-d-3)}\right)^3 * (n-2) * (n-3) \tag{4.3.11}$$

$n-2$ and $n-3$ are multiplied in the above equation, as the two intermediate nodes can be any of the rest of $n-2$ and $n-3$ nodes of the network.

4.3.1 Expressing Probability in terms of Total Nodes

The average degree of nodes can be expressed in terms of total number of community members. Let $d = n/k$, where k is a constant. If k=1, then community is a clique.

Chapter 4. *Community Detection in Social Networks Based on Fire Propagation*

Replacing the value of $d = n/k$ in equations 4.3.7 and 4.3.10:

$$P_1 = \frac{\frac{n^2}{k^2}}{\frac{n^2}{k^2} + \frac{(k-1)^2}{k^2} * n^2}$$

$$\Rightarrow P_1 \geq \frac{1}{k^2 - 2k + 2} \tag{4.3.12}$$

Similarly,

$$P_2 \geq \frac{n-2}{(k^2 - 2k + 2)^2} \tag{4.3.13}$$

Therefore, the probability of two nodes belonging to a community, connected directly in a two-radius neighborhood graph $= P = P_1 + P_2$ and the value of P can be written as:

$$P \geq \frac{1}{k^2 - 2k + 2} + \frac{n-2}{(k^2 - 2k + 2)^2} \tag{4.3.14}$$

If 3-radius neighborhood is considered for the process, then the equation 4.3.14 has to be modified as:

$$P \geq \frac{1}{k^2 - 2k + 2} + \frac{n-2}{(k^2 - 2k + 2)^2} + \frac{(n-2)(n-3)}{(k^2 - 2k + 2)^3} \tag{4.3.15}$$

For this work, the value of k is assumed to be 3.0. However, this work can be easily modified for $k \geq 3$ or $d \leq \frac{n}{3}$.

4.3.2 Relation Between Community Size and Edge Density

Let, C be a community of size n. The edge density of the community is defined in terms of k; as $d = n/k$. Replacing the value of $k = 2$ in equation 4.3.14:

$$P \geq \frac{1}{2^2 - 2*2 + 2} + \frac{n-2}{(2^2 - 2*2 + 2)^2}$$

$$\Rightarrow P \geq \frac{1}{2} + \frac{n-2}{4}$$

If P is asuumed to be 1.0, then

$$\frac{1}{2} + \frac{n-2}{4} = 1$$

$$\Rightarrow \frac{n-2}{4} = 0.5$$

$$\Rightarrow n = 0.5 * 4 + 2 = 4$$

Putting the value of $k = 3$ in equation 4.3.14:

$$P \geq \frac{1}{3^2 - 2*3 + 2} + \frac{n-2}{(3^2 - 2*3 + 2)^2}$$

$$\Rightarrow P \geq \frac{1}{5} + \frac{n-2}{25}$$

If P is asuumed to be 1.0, then

$$\frac{1}{5} + \frac{n-2}{25} = 1$$

$$\Rightarrow \frac{n-2}{25} = 0.8$$

$$\Rightarrow n = 0.8 * 25 + 2 = 22$$

Similarly, replacing k=3 in equation 4.3.15:

$$P \geq \frac{1}{3^2 - 2*3 + 2} + \frac{n-2}{(3^2 - 2*3 + 2)^2} + \frac{(n-2)(n-3)}{(3^2 - 2*3 + 2)^2}$$

$$\Rightarrow P \geq \frac{1}{5} + \frac{n-2}{25} + \frac{(n-2)(n-3)}{125}$$

If P is asuumed to be 1.0, then

$$P \geq \frac{1}{5} + \frac{n-2}{25} + \frac{(n-2)(n-3)}{125}$$

$$\Rightarrow \frac{n-2}{25} + \frac{(n-2)(n-3)}{125} = 0.8$$

$$\Rightarrow 5(n-2) + (n-2)(n-3) = 0.8 * 125$$

$$\Rightarrow (n-2)(n+2) = 100$$

$$\Rightarrow n = 9.797 \approx 10$$

Theorem 4.3.1. For a community C of size n and average node degree $d = n/2$; if $n \geq 4$, then a two-radius neighborhood subgraph of a member node is enough to search for all nodes of C.

Corollary 4.3.2. For a community C of size n and average node degree $d = n/3$; if $n \geq 22$, then a two-radius neighborhood subgraph of a member node is enough to search for all nodes of C.

Corollary 4.3.3. For a community C of size n and average node degree $d = n/3$; if $n \geq 10$, then a three-radius neighborhood subgraph of a member node is enough to search for all nodes of C.

4.4 Proposed Fire Spread Algorithm

The proposed Fire Spread algorithm works in two phases. In the first phase, the algorithm starts with a random node in the network as a seed node and finds a two-radius neighborhood subgraph. The two-radius neighborhood subgraph is a subgraph which includes the seed node, its immediate neighbors, and neighbor nodes of its neighbors. In the second phase, the algorithm finds the community structure around the seed from the two-radius neighborhood subgraph using Fire Spread model. The algorithm repetitively chooses seed nodes and detects communities around those seed nodes. The proposed algorithm executes until all the nodes of the network become part of at least one of the communities. The algorithm is not limited to work only with two-radius neighborhood subgraphs; it can work with R-radius neighborhood subgraph (for any integer value of R) if the chosen network is sparse.

4.4.1 Two Radius Neighborhood Subgraph

As already discussed in section 4.1; finding communities in a social network is an NP-hard problem. Any group of nodes forming a clique between themselves is always the best choice to be identified as a community. A clique is a subgraph in which direct-edges connect all the nodes. However, inside a functional community, all these nodes are not connected directly, forming a clique. Hence, the criteria of communities to be cliques is relaxed in this work. It is assumed that the members of a community are connected directly to at least one-third members of the community.

For a community C with n number of nodes; it is assumed that, $d \geq n/3$, where d is the average degree of nodes inside the community C.

The proposed algorithm is designed to find communities locally using a greedy method to reduce time complexity. The proposed algorithm selects a seed node s and extracts a two-radius neighborhood sub-graph g. The subgraph g is then used to search for community. If the social network graph has an average node degree d, then with two-radius neighborhood, it will search among $O(d^2)$ nodes instead of total network of N nodes.

4.4.2 Modeling Fire Spread Algorithm

The proposed algorithm is a nature inspired algorithm, which takes its motivation from spreading of fire in real-world scenarios. Fire spread from a source is a similar kind of phenomena as community detection. Fire starts from a source and spread to other areas. A neighbor near to a source can catch fire which depends on heat transmission coefficient (T_h) between the source and its neighbor. Hence, it can be assumed that probability of catching fire (P_i) near a source is directly proportional to heat transmission coefficient (T_h).

$$P \propto T_h \qquad (4.4.1)$$

Therefore, $P = KT_h$, where K is a constant.

Similarly a place, which has most of its neighbors caught in fire, is most likely to catch fire. If a point i has n of its neighboring nodes caught fire then probability of catching fire (P_i) at point i can be represented as:

$$P_i = P_{i|1} + P_{i|2} + P_{i|3} + \cdots + P_{i|n-1} + P_{i|n} \tag{4.4.2}$$

where $P_{i|1}, P_{i|2}, P_{i|3}, \ldots P_{i|n-1}, P_{i|n}$ are probabilities of catching fire at point i due to $1^{st}, 2^{nd}, 3^{rd} \ldots n-1^{th}, n^{th}$ neighbors respectively.

The fire catching probability at point i is denoted as P_i and it depends on fire probability $P_{i|j} \ \forall j \in neighbor(i)$.

From equation 4.4.1 and equation 4.4.2, P_i can be derived as:

$$P_i = \sum_{j \in N(i)} P_{i|j} = \sum_{j \in N(i)} P_j * KT_{hj} \tag{4.4.3}$$

where K is a constant, T_{hj} = heat transfer coefficient for j^{th} neighbor and P_j is probability of fire at j^{th} neighbor. K is assumed to be fixed with value 1.0 for all the networks.

4.4.3 Threshold to Catch Fire

Each material has its combustion temperature t, beyond which it will catch fire. In the proposed algorithm, a threshold value is defined to observe the status (if the node catches fire not) of the node. Less the value of the threshold, more is the probability of catching fire.

A binary function Fire(), that takes decisions based on threshold values of the nodes, is defined by equation 4.4.4.

$$Fire(i) = \begin{cases} 1 & \text{if } P_i \geq Threshold_i \\ 0 & \text{if } P_i < Threshold_i \end{cases} \tag{4.4.4}$$

4.4.4 Designing the Proposed Algorithm

Finding community using the proposed FSA is centered around finding clusters near random seed nodes. The algorithm starts detecting communities near specified seed nodes, that are randomly chosen. The selected seed nodes are those nodes which are not already a part of any of the detected communities. Unlike some other algorithms, there is no need to give the number of communities explicitly. The seed node is assumed to be the source of fire in real-world scenarios. The fire catching probability, $P_{seed} = 1$, is set for the seed node. Neighbor nodes of the seed node are set with the probability of catching fire P_j, using equation 4.4.2. P_j takes different values for each node. Since un-weighted and undirected graphs are used in this work, the distance of a node from the seed node

Chapter 4. Community Detection in Social Networks Based on Fire Propagation

is expressed in terms of edge distance. Nodes which are adjacent to seed nodes are more likely to catch fire (originating from the seed). As the distance from the seed node to a specific node increases, the fire catching probability decreases.

A node which has a high number of its adjacent nodes in the fire, is more probable of catching fire, as described in equation 4.4.2. A threshold value is defined for each node, which decides whether the concerned node catches fire or not. The threshold value will be different for each node. A node which has less degree is more likely to be the part of a community, compared to a node which has a higher degree, since the high-degree node has a higher probability of being a part of some other communities as well.

$$Threshold_i \propto Degree(i) \qquad (4.4.5)$$

Community membership value, calculated using equation 4.4.4, resembles with the fire spreading phenomenon. A node which catches fire due to a seed (source) node most likely belongs to the community to which the seed node is also a member. A node which catches fire due to a specific seed node can also catch fire due to another seed node. This property is used to define shared communities in which more than one nodes are shared between two communities.

4.4.4.1 Finding Shared Communities

Most of the community detection algorithms are not efficient in finding shared communities, though they can find hierarchical community structures. Moreover, some of the shared community detection algorithms take the total number of communities as a parameter. However, this number cannot be predicted efficiently before the execution of the method. The proposed method does not require the total number of communities before executing the algorithm. It dynamically detects the shared communities depending on the network structure. The proposed FSA is based on the idea that, if two communities C_1 and C_2 are two distinct communities, then there must be at least one node in C_1 which is not present in C_2 and vice-versa. If $C_1 \not\subset C_2$ and $C_2 \not\subset C_1$, then $C1$ and $C2$ are different communities.

4.4.4.2 Distance and Probability Relation

The following formulation relates the fire-catching probability of a node and its distance from the seed:

$$P_i \propto (p_{avg})^{distance} \qquad (4.4.6)$$

Chapter 4. *Community Detection in Social Networks Based on Fire Propagation* 52

where P_i is the probability of catching fire at node i, p_{avg} is the average fire propagation probability of the network, which is calculated as follows:

$$p_{avg} = \frac{1}{\text{average degree of two-radius neighborhood graph}} \quad (4.4.7)$$

Since $p_{avg} \leq 1$, the value of P decreases exponentially with distance.

4.4.4.3 Fire Propagation Probability for each Node

Equation 4.4.8 gives the fire propagation probability p_i for node i with degree d_i.

$$Fire\ Propagation\ Probability\ (p_i) = \frac{1}{d_i} \quad (4.4.8)$$

The fire propagation probability (p_i) is equivalent to heat transfer coefficient (T_h), described in equation 4.3.16.

4.4.4.4 Expected Number of Nodes of a Community

Let, g be a two-radius neighborhood subgraph of G with n nodes and e edges. Though the community is contained in subgraph g, not all n nodes of g are part of the community. Hence, there is a requirement to find the fraction of nodes of g, likely to be part of the community. This value, can be denoted as $multi\_factor_1$ (multiplication factor 1), given by equation 4.4.9.

$$multi\_factor_1 = \frac{E'}{E' + 2e} \quad (4.4.9)$$

where e is number of edges of subgraph g and E' is total number of edges connecting a node inside g to a node outside g. The $multi\_factor_1$ is multiplied with the number of nodes of the two-radius neighborhood subgraph g, to calculate the expected number of nodes of the community. The number of nodes selected for a community is inversely proportional to the value of $multi\_factor_1$.

A higher degree node is more likely to be selected as a community member since it is having more links than a lesser degree node. A node having less degree with most of its links lie inside the community, should be given priority in comparison with a higher degree node having most of its links to outside. Therefore, a second multiplication factor is multiplied, which is denoted as $multi\_factor_2$, given by equation 4.4.10.

$$multi\_factor_2 = \frac{G.degree(i)}{g.degree(i)} \quad (4.4.10)$$

where g is the two-radius neighborhood subgraph of graph G.

4.4.4.5 Calculation of Threshold Value

To calculate the expected value of threshold of a node, belonging to the community, average fire propagation probability (p_{avg}) is required, which is defined by equation 4.4.11.

$$p_{avg} = \sum_{\forall i \in g} \frac{1}{G.degree(i)} \qquad (4.4.11)$$

where g is a two-radius neighborhood subgraph of G.

As already discussed, it is assumed that the average node degree $d = n/k$, where $k = 3$. Let, n' be the expected number of nodes of the community and n'_1 be the expected number of nodes directly connected to the seed node. The value of n'_1 is defined as:

$$n'_1 = P_1 * n' \qquad (4.4.12)$$

where P_1 is the probability of direct-edge between any two nodes, belonging to the same community. The value of P_1 is calculated using equation 4.3.5.

Similarly, the expected numbers of nodes, connected through an intermediate node to the seed node, denoted as n_2', is given by equation 4.4.13.

$$n_2' = P_2 * n' \qquad (4.4.13)$$

where P_2 is the probability of connection between any two community member nodes through an intermediate node. The value of P_2 is calculated using equation 4.3.10.

However, the number of nodes of a community (n') cannot be calculated before the community is detected. Therefore, this value is approximated from the number of nodes of two-radius neighborhood subgraph using equation 4.4.14.

$$n' \approx n * multi\_factor_1 \qquad (4.4.14)$$

where, n = number of nodes of two-radius neighborhood subgraph g and the value of $multi\_factor_1$ is calculated using equation 4.4.9.

A member of the community is likely to be connected with n'/k nodes of the community through direct-edges. Among these connected nodes, some will be at a 1-edge distance from the seed and others will be at a 2-edge distance. These numbers are already defined in equation 4.4.12 and 4.4.13.

Chapter 4. *Community Detection in Social Networks Based on Fire Propagation*

Fire_Spread(G, R):
Data : Graph G, Radius R
Result: List of communities
$List1 = [\,]$ ▶ Blank list to store community nodes.
$List2 = [\,]$ ▶ Blank list to store communities.
while *node $i \in G$* do
    if $i \notin List2$ then
        $g = G.Neighborhood\_subgraph(G, i, R)$
        $List1 = Local\_Fire\_Spread(G, g, i)$
        $List2.append(List1)$
    end
end
return $List2$

Algorithm 1: Fire Spread Algorithm

The value of threshold, used to calculate membership of a node, is the expected value of fire catching probability of a community node. The threshold value of node i is given by equation 4.4.15.

$$Threshold(i) = ((n'_1 * p_{avg} + n'_2 * p^2_{avg}) * p_{avg} * \frac{1}{k}) * multi\_factor_2 \quad (4.4.15)$$

where i is a node inside subgraph g, whose threshold value is calculated, $n=$ number of nodes of g, value of $k = 3$ and $multi\_factor_2$ is calculated using equation 4.4.10.

Similarly, for three-radius neighborhood subgraph having $k = 3$, threshold value is calculated as:

$$Threshold(i) = ((n'_1 * p_{avg} + n'_2 * p^2_{avg} + n'_3 * p^3_{avg}) * p_{avg} * \frac{1}{k}) * multi\_factor_2 \quad (4.4.16)$$

where $n'_3 = n' * P_3$

4.4.5 Fire Spread Community Detection Algorithm

The proposed Fire Spread algorithm (FSA) is divided in to two parts. The first part of the algorithm is a local community detection algorithm, which requires a seed node and its R-radius neighborhood subgraph as input. Second part of the algorithm is a global community detection algorithm. This algorithm takes the whole network as an argument. It discovers the communities by selecting random seed nodes, calculating R-radius neighborhood subgraph of those seeds, and calls the local community detection algorithm with chosen seed nodes and their R-radius neighborhood subgraphs.

Local_Fire_Spread(G, g, s):
Data: Graph G, Subgraph g, Seed s
Result: List of community nodes
$List = [\,]$ ▶ Blank list to store community nodes.
while *Node i in g* **do**
    if $i{==}s$ **then**
        $P_s = 1.0$
        $p_s = 1.0$
    else
        $P_i = 0.0$
        $p_i = 1/G.degree(i)$
    end
end
while *node* $i \in g$ **do**
    while *node* $j \in g.Neighbor(i)$ **do**
        $P_{i|j} = P_j \times p_i$
        $P_{j|i} = P_i \times p_j$
        $P_i = P_i + P_{i|j}$
        $P_j = P_j + P_{j|i}$
    end
end
while *node* $i \in g$ **do**
    if $P_i \geq Threshold(G, g, i)$ **then**
        $List.append(i)$
    end
end
return *List*

Algorithm 2: Local Fire Spread Algorithm

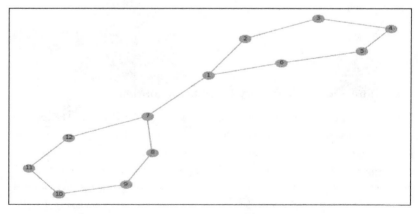

Figure 4.8: Graph Before Execution of Fire Spread Algorithm

An Example:

Threshold(G, g, i):
Data : Graph G, Subgraph g, Node i
Result: Threshold value for node i
$n = g.Number-of-nodes()$
$e = g.Number-of-Edges()$
$k = n^2/2.0 \times e$
$p_{avg} = 0.0$
while $node\ j \in g$ **do**
$\quad\mid\ p_{avg} = p_{avg} + G.Degree(j)$
end
$p_{avg} = \frac{p_{avg}}{g.Number-of-Nodes()}$
$E = 0$
while $node\ j \in g$ **do**
$\quad\mid\ E = E + (G.Degree(j) - g.Degree(j))$
end
$mf_1 = \frac{E}{E+2\times g.Number-of-Edges()}$ ▶
$n' = g.Number-of-Nodes() \times mf_1$ ▶
$Prob_1 = \frac{1}{k^2-2k+2}$ ▶
$Prob_2 = \frac{n-2}{(k^2-2k+2)^2}$ ▶
$n'_1 = Prob_1 \times n'$ ▶
$n'_2 = Prob_2 \times n'$ ▶
$mf_2 = \frac{G.Degree(i)}{g.Degree(i)}$ ▶
$Thres = ((n'_1 \times p_{avg} + n'_2 \times p_{avg}^2) \times p_{avg} \times \frac{1}{k}) \times mf_2$ ▶
return $Thres$

Algorithm 3: Algorithm To Calculate Threshold

To explain the execution of the algorithm, a graph with 12 nodes and 13 edges is generated, shown in Figure 4.8. The graph has two communities; each is having 6 nodes, connected by an edge $(1, 7)$. The algorithm is executed locally to detect community involving nodes $(1, 2, 3, 4, 5, 6)$. The two extreme cases of community detection are considered here; the first one using node 4 as seed and the second one using node 1 as seed. The community detected with seed 4 is shown in Figure 4.9 (blue colored). Similarly, the community detected with seed 1 is shown in Figure 4.10. Since the communities are sparse, so 4-radius neighborhood subgraph is used in the first stage of the algorithm.

4.4.5.1 Complexity of Fire Spread Algorithm

The proposed algorithm is modeled by modifying the Breadth First Search (BFS) algorithm, so the time complexity of the proposed algorithm is same with BFS at the local level. For finding a community near any seed node, the algorithm is provided with a two-radius neighborhood subgraph as input. If the social network graph has an average node degree d_{avg}, then with a two-radius neighborhood subgraph, the algorithm would search among $O(d_{avg}^2)$ nodes instead of an entire network of N nodes. Hence, the complexity of the algorithm at the local level surrounding a seed node is $O(e + v)$, where e is the

Chapter 4. Community Detection in Social Networks Based on Fire Propagation

average number of edges and v is average numbers of nodes per two-radius neighborhood subgraph. If the social network constitutes l communities, the overall time complexity of the network becomes $= O(l(e + v))$.

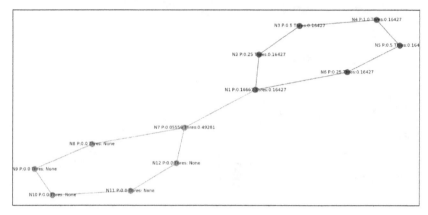

Figure 4.9: Community Detected with Node4 as Seed

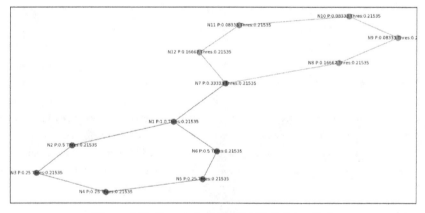

Figure 4.10: Community Detected with Node1 as Seed

4.4.6 Predicting the Radius of a Community

The Fire spread community detection algorithm is executed with radius value 2, 3 and 4. By executing the FS algorithm for various networks, the above-mentioned radius values found to be optimal. However, the accuracy of the algorithm is highly dependent on setting of radius values. In this section, the radius value of the community is automatically set. For localization of community detection, determining the radius of a community is vital. However, until the community is detected, determining the exact value of radius is impossible, though predicting the radius of a community using the probabilistic method is possible. For predicting the radius, a random seed node is picked, and a 2-neighborhood (neighbor of the neighbor of the seed) subgraph around the seed is found. The local information collected from the subgraph is used to predict the radius of the community. For the prediction of radius, we assume that the community as a subgraph is connected; any two nodes inside the community have a path between them, which is less than or equal to the radius r.

The degrees of all the nodes of the 2-neighborhood subgraph are stored in a list from which the probability of edges between each pair of nodes is calculated based on the degrees of the nodes. A pair of nodes with higher degrees are more likely to be linked by an edge than a pair of nodes with lesser degrees. For a 2-neighborhood subgraph g, let L be the list where the node degrees are stored. Without considering the actual edge between the vertices of g, the probability of edges between each pair of node is calculated using equation 4.3.3 and stored in a matrix A. Matrix A is of dimension $n \times n$, where n is the number of nodes of g. In each step of the algorithm, the probability of a shortest path with particular hop-count is predicted. As we have assumed that a community is connected itself. Therefore each node has a path to other nodes in the subgraph g, which is denoted as probability 1.0. The path probability matrix in each step is calculated based on the values of the previous step. Matrix A is the initial path probability matrix with path length 1. The algorithm stops, when the matrix storing the probability of path between each pair of nodes has all its entries approximately 1.0. The value of that particular step is the radius of the graph.

Let $node_i$ and $node_j$ are the nodes whose degrees are stored at i^{th} and j^{th} locations respectively, in L. The entry $A[i][j]$ defines the probability of edge between $node_i$ and $node_j$ and is defined as:

$$A[i][j] = \begin{cases} \frac{\frac{(n-2)}{(L[i]-1)} \times \frac{(n-2)}{(L[j]-1)}}{\frac{(n-2)}{(L[i]-1)} \times \frac{(n-2)}{(L[j]-1)} + \frac{(n-2)}{L[i]} \times \frac{(n-2)}{L[j]}} & \text{if } i \neq j \\ 0.0 & \text{if } i = j \end{cases} \quad (4.4.17)$$

The value of $A[i][i] = 0.0$ signifies the zero probability of self-edge as self-edges are not considered. Row_i of matrix A stores the probabilities of edges between $node_i$ and the other nodes. The summation of all the entries of Row_i is the expected degree of $node_i$, and it should be equal to $L[i]$, which is the actual degree of the node. The probability of an edge between each pair of nodes defined in equation 4.4.17 is not the actual probability but only an initial value, and it has to be normalized. The entries of matrix A are normalized so that the summation of the entries of Row_i is equal to $L[i]$. The values of Row_i are normalized, and the entries are updated as:

$$A[i][j] = \frac{A[i][j] * L[i]}{sum_i} \qquad (4.4.18)$$

where sum_i is the summation of all the entries of Row_i.

Matrix A^2 is calculated by multiplying A with itself. Any of the entries of A^2, denoted as $A^2[i][j]$, is calculated as $\sum_{t=1}^{t=n} A[i][t] * A[t][j]$, which corresponds to a path between i^{th} node and j^{th} node through t^{th} intermediate node. The tth intermediate node can be any of the n nodes (except for $t = i$ and $t = j$). Evidently, the value of $A^2[i][j]$ corresponds to the probability of a 2-length path between i^{th} node and j^{th} node. Similarly, the entries of A^k correspond to the probability of k-length paths between the node pairs. However, computing the probability of shortest path of length k must exclude the probability of shortest path having length less than k.

A matrix I with dimensions $n \times n$ is defined for the probability of path between any two nodes of g. Therefore, all the entries of I are set to 1.0 (we are assuming the communities as connected).

Another matrix B^k with dimensions $n \times n$ is defined which stores the probability of path between each pair of nodes of g with k being the maximum allowed distance between nodes. B^1 is initialized to A. Matrix A^k is also defined as A multiplied k times. A matrix R^K of dimensions $n \times n$ is used to store the residual probability of nodes, i,e, the probability of having a shortest path with distance $>= k$. R^1 is initialized to I. Matrix R^k is calculated as:

$$R^k = \begin{cases} I - B^{k-1} & \text{for } k \geq 2 \\ I & \text{for } k = 1 \end{cases} \qquad (4.4.19)$$

The value of $B[i][j]$ is calculated as:

$$B^k = \begin{cases} B^{k-1} + (A^k \times R^k) & \text{for } k \geq 2 \\ A & \text{for } k = 1 \end{cases} \qquad (4.4.20)$$

In the above equation the multiplication between A^k and R^k is not a matrix multiplication, rather $A^k[i][j]$ is directly multiplied with $R^k[i][j]$.

In each step, for $k <= n$, all the entries of R^{k+1} are added. If the addition result is approximately equal to zero, then the entries of B^k are very closed to 1.0, and the entries

find_radius (g):
Data: Graph instance g
Result: Radius r
$n =$ number of nodes of g and $e =$ number of edges of g
$L[1 \ldots n] =$ degree of node of g and $A[1 \ldots n][1 \ldots n] = [\ ][\ ]$
Initialize $A[i][j] = \dfrac{\frac{(n-2)}{(L[i]-1)} \times \frac{(n-2)}{(L[j]-1)}}{\frac{(n-2)}{(L[i]-1)} \times \frac{(n-2)}{(L[j]-1)} + \frac{(n-2)}{L[i]} \times \frac{(n-2)}{L[j]}}$ for $i \neq j$ and 0.0 for $i == j$
while i ranges from 1 to n **do**
$sum = 0.0$
while j ranges from 1 to n **do**
$sum = sum + A[i][j]$
end
while j ranges from 1 to n **do**
$A[i][j] = \frac{A[i][j] * L[i]}{sum}$
end
end
$I[1 \ldots n][1 \ldots n] =$ Set all entries to 1.0
$B^1[1 \ldots n][1 \ldots n] = A$, $R^1[1 \ldots n][1 \ldots n] = I$
if $\sum_{i=1}^{i=n} \sum_{j=1}^{j=n} B^1[i][j] \approx n(n-1)$ **then**
return 1
end
while i ranges from 2 to n **do**
$A^k = A^{k-1} \times A$ and $R^k = I - B^{k-1}$
$B^k = B^{k-1} + A^k \times R^k$
if $\sum_{i=1}^{i=n} \sum_{j=1}^{j=n} R^k[i][j] \approx 0.0$ **then**
return k
end
end

Algorithm 4: Algorithm to Predict the Radius of a Community

of R^{k+1} are very closed to 0.0, which signifies each pair of nodes have the shortest path between them having a distance less than or equal to k. The corresponding value of k is approximated as the radius r of the community.

Example

In order to explain the prediction of diameter, the karate club graph [**Zachary** (1977)] is taken as an example. Arbitrarily, node 24 is selected as seed node. The nodes of the 2-neighborhood subgraph of node 24 are: $[0, 33, 2, 32, 23, 24, 25, 27, 28, 31]$

The initial matrix entries of A or A^1 are computed using equation 4.4.17 and normalized using equation 4.4.18. After normalization, matrix A^1, which represents the probability of edges between the nodes, is given in Table 4.3.

Matrix B^1, which stores the probability of path between nodes, with 1 being the

Chapter 4. *Community Detection in Social Networks Based on Fire Propagation* 61

Table 4.3: Path Probability matrix A for Node 24

0.0	0.278	0.222	0.222	0.222	0.167	0.167	0.222	0.167	0.333
0.303	0.0	0.606	0.606	0.606	0.455	0.455	0.606	0.455	0.909
0.235	0.588	0.0	0.471	0.471	0.353	0.353	0.471	0.353	0.706
0.235	0.588	0.471	0.0	0.471	0.353	0.353	0.471	0.353	0.706
0.235	0.588	0.471	0.471	0.0	0.353	0.353	0.471	0.353	0.706
0.171	0.429	0.343	0.343	0.343	0.0	0.257	0.343	0.257	0.514
0.171	0.429	0.343	0.343	0.343	0.257	0.0	0.343	0.257	0.514
0.235	0.588	0.471	0.471	0.471	0.353	0.353	0.0	0.353	0.706
0.171	0.429	0.343	0.343	0.343	0.257	0.257	0.343	0.0	0.514
0.375	0.937	0.75	0.75	0.75	0.563	0.563	0.75	0.562	0.0

Table 4.4: Residual Probability Matrix R^2

0.0	0.722	0.778	0.778	0.778	0.833	0.833	0.778	0.833	0.667
0.697	0.0	0.394	0.394	0.394	0.545	0.545	0.394	0.545	0.091
0.765	0.412	0.0	0.529	0.529	0.647	0.647	0.529	0.647	0.294
0.765	0.412	0.529	0.0	0.529	0.647	0.647	0.529	0.647	0.294
0.765	0.412	0.529	0.529	0.0	0.647	0.647	0.529	0.647	0.294
0.829	0.571	0.657	0.657	0.657	0.0	0.743	0.657	0.743	0.486
0.829	0.571	0.657	0.657	0.657	0.743	0.0	0.657	0.743	0.486
0.765	0.412	0.529	0.529	0.529	0.647	0.647	0.0	0.647	0.294
0.829	0.571	0.657	0.657	0.657	0.743	0.743	0.657	0.0	0.486
0.625	0.063	0.25	0.25	0.25	0.438	0.438	0.25	0.438	0.0

Table 4.5: Probability of 2-length Path A^2

0.0	0.722	0.703	0.703	0.703	0.594	0.594	0.703	0.594	0.667
0.697	0.0	0.394	0.394	0.394	0.545	0.545	0.394	0.545	0.091
0.732	0.412	0.0	0.529	0.529	0.647	0.647	0.529	0.647	0.294
0.732	0.412	0.529	0.0	0.529	0.647	0.647	0.529	0.647	0.294
0.732	0.412	0.529	0.529	0.0	0.647	0.647	0.529	0.647	0.294
0.608	0.571	0.657	0.657	0.657	0.0	0.743	0.657	0.743	0.486
0.608	0.571	0.657	0.657	0.657	0.743	0.0	0.657	0.743	0.486
0.732	0.412	0.529	0.529	0.529	0.647	0.647	0.0	0.647	0.294
0.608	0.571	0.657	0.657	0.657	0.743	0.743	0.657	0.0	0.486
0.625	0.063	0.25	0.25	0.25	0.438	0.438	0.25	0.438	0.0

maximum allowed path length, is same as A^1. Entries of Residual probability matrix R^1 (stores probability of shortest path with path length greater than 0) are 1.0, with diagonal entries set to 0.0. The entries of residual probability matrix R^2 (stores probability of shortest path with path length greater than 1) are calculated by subtracting each entry of B^1 from 1.0, except the diagonal entries. Matrix R^2 is given in Table 4.4.

Matrix A^2 which stores the probability of 2-length paths between nodes is calculated by matrix A multiplied with itself. The entries of matrix A^2 are in Table 4.5:

Table 4.6: Probabilty of 2-length Shotest Paths B^2

0.0	1.0	0.925	0.925	0.925	0.761	0.761	0.925	0.761	1.0
1.0	0.0	1.0	1.0	1.0	1.0	1.0	1.0	1.0	1.0
0.967	1.0	0.0	1.0	1.0	1.0	1.0	1.0	1.0	1.0
0.967	1.0	1.0	0.0	1.0	1.0	1.0	1.0	1.0	1.0
0.967	1.0	1.0	1.0	0.0	1.0	1.0	1.0	1.0	1.0
0.779	1.0	1.0	1.0	1.0	0.0	1.0	1.0	1.0	1.0
0.779	1.0	1.0	1.0	1.0	1.0	0.0	1.0	1.0	1.0
0.967	1.0	1.0	1.0	1.0	1.0	1.0	0.0	1.0	1.0
0.779	1.0	1.0	1.0	1.0	1.0	1.0	1.0	0.0	1.0
1.0	1.0	1.0	1.0	1.0	1.0	1.0	1.0	1.0	0.0

Table 4.7: Residul Probability Matrix R^3

0.0	0.0	0.075	0.075	0.075	0.239	0.239	0.075	0.239	0.0
0.0	0.0	0.0	0.0	0.0	0.0	0.0	0.0	0.0	0.0
0.033	0.0	0.0	0.0	0.0	0.0	0.0	0.0	0.0	0.0
0.033	0.0	0.0	0.0	0.0	0.0	0.0	0.0	0.0	0.0
0.033	0.0	0.0	0.0	0.0	0.0	0.0	0.0	0.0	0.0
0.221	0.0	0.0	0.0	0.0	0.0	0.0	0.0	0.0	0.0
0.221	0.0	0.0	0.0	0.0	0.0	0.0	0.0	0.0	0.0
0.033	0.0	0.0	0.0	0.0	0.0	0.0	0.0	0.0	0.0
0.221	0.0	0.0	0.0	0.0	0.0	0.0	0.0	0.0	0.0
0.0	0.0	0.0	0.0	0.0	0.0	0.0	0.0	0.0	0.0

Matrix B^2, which stores the probability of path between nodes with a maximum allowed path length 2, is calculated as $B^1 + A^2 \times R^2$. Here, each entry of $A^2[i][j]$ is multiplied with each entry of $R^2[i][j]$. Matrix B^2 is given in Table 4.6.

The residual matrix R^3 (stores the probability of path with path length greater than 2) is calculated by subtracting each entry of B^2 from 1.0, except the diagonal entries, is given in Table 4.7. The matrices A^3, B^3 and R^4 are also calculated as explained in the previous steps. Matrix B^3, which stores the probability of path between nodes with maximal allowed path length being 3, is given in Table 4.8. The residual probability matrix R^4, which stores the probability of shortest path with path length greater than 3 is given in Table 4.9.

It can be seen that, each entry of R^4 is 0.0. This implies that the shortest path lengths will have length less than or equal to 3. Therefore, the predicted radius is 3.

4.5 Chapter Summary

We proposed a novel, nature-inspired, Fire Spread algorithm to detect communities in social networks. The proposed algorithm is based on the spread of fire starting from a

Chapter 4. *Community Detection in Social Networks Based on Fire Propagation* 63

Table 4.8: Probability of 3-length Shortest Path B^3

$$\begin{vmatrix} 0.0 & 1.0 & 1.0 & 1.0 & 1.0 & 1.0 & 1.0 & 1.0 & 1.0 & 1.0 \\ 1.0 & 0.0 & 1.0 & 1.0 & 1.0 & 1.0 & 1.0 & 1.0 & 1.0 & 1.0 \\ 1.0 & 1.0 & 0.0 & 1.0 & 1.0 & 1.0 & 1.0 & 1.0 & 1.0 & 1.0 \\ 1.0 & 1.0 & 1.0 & 0.0 & 1.0 & 1.0 & 1.0 & 1.0 & 1.0 & 1.0 \\ 1.0 & 1.0 & 1.0 & 1.0 & 0.0 & 1.0 & 1.0 & 1.0 & 1.0 & 1.0 \\ 1.0 & 1.0 & 1.0 & 1.0 & 1.0 & 0.0 & 1.0 & 1.0 & 1.0 & 1.0 \\ 1.0 & 1.0 & 1.0 & 1.0 & 1.0 & 1.0 & 0.0 & 1.0 & 1.0 & 1.0 \\ 1.0 & 1.0 & 1.0 & 1.0 & 1.0 & 1.0 & 1.0 & 0.0 & 1.0 & 1.0 \\ 1.0 & 1.0 & 1.0 & 1.0 & 1.0 & 1.0 & 1.0 & 1.0 & 0.0 & 1.0 \\ 1.0 & 1.0 & 1.0 & 1.0 & 1.0 & 1.0 & 1.0 & 1.0 & 1.0 & 0.0 \end{vmatrix}$$

Table 4.9: Residual Probabilty Matrix R^4

$$\begin{vmatrix} 0.0 & 0.0 & 0.0 & 0.0 & 0.0 & 0.0 & 0.0 & 0.0 & 0.0 & 0.0 \\ 0.0 & 0.0 & 0.0 & 0.0 & 0.0 & 0.0 & 0.0 & 0.0 & 0.0 & 0.0 \\ 0.0 & 0.0 & 0.0 & 0.0 & 0.0 & 0.0 & 0.0 & 0.0 & 0.0 & 0.0 \\ 0.0 & 0.0 & 0.0 & 0.0 & 0.0 & 0.0 & 0.0 & 0.0 & 0.0 & 0.0 \\ 0.0 & 0.0 & 0.0 & 0.0 & 0.0 & 0.0 & 0.0 & 0.0 & 0.0 & 0.0 \\ 0.0 & 0.0 & 0.0 & 0.0 & 0.0 & 0.0 & 0.0 & 0.0 & 0.0 & 0.0 \\ 0.0 & 0.0 & 0.0 & 0.0 & 0.0 & 0.0 & 0.0 & 0.0 & 0.0 & 0.0 \\ 0.0 & 0.0 & 0.0 & 0.0 & 0.0 & 0.0 & 0.0 & 0.0 & 0.0 & 0.0 \\ 0.0 & 0.0 & 0.0 & 0.0 & 0.0 & 0.0 & 0.0 & 0.0 & 0.0 & 0.0 \\ 0.0 & 0.0 & 0.0 & 0.0 & 0.0 & 0.0 & 0.0 & 0.0 & 0.0 & 0.0 \end{vmatrix}$$

source. We proved that a two-radius neighborhood graph is enough to search for local community around a seed node if each node in the community is connected to at least one-third of nodes inside the community. Therefore, the proposed algorithm works with two-radius/three-radius neighborhood subgraphs, to minimize the search space. However, it must be noted that the algorithm can work with r-radius neighborhood for any integer value of r, not just with a two-radius neighborhood. A novel probability based algorithm is designed, which is capable of finding the radius of community, given a seed node. This is used to automate the setting of radius values for proposed FSA. Moreover, the radius prediction algorithm can be used with any of the exiting community detection algorithms to localize the community detection.

The proposed algorithm can work both at the local level with a specific seed node, and at network level by automatically selecting random seed nodes. The proposed algorithm performs efficiently even in the presence of shared communities. By controlling the threshold value, the proposed Fire Spread algorithm can detect multiple-resolution hierarchical community structures. The FSA does not require a predefined value for the total number of communities of a network. In addition to this, the algorithm can assign a single node to more than one communities, if the concerned node is shared between different communities.

Chapter 5

COMPARISON OF FSA WITH OTHER COMMUNITY DETECTION ALGORITHMS

5.1 Outline

The results of proposed FSA is described in five sections. Firstly, the proposed FSA is evaluated in terms of recall and precision with respect to predefined community membership values, using both real-world and synthetic datasets, described in section 5.2. Further, the impact of distinct seed nodes on recall and precision values by employing local_FSA is discussed in section 5.3. The proposed community detection algorithm can detect multiple-resolution community structure in a network and is explained in section 5.4. The performance evaluation of the proposed algorithm in terms of modularity and conductance is conducted in section 5.5, by comparing it with some of the state-of-the-art community detection algorithms, viz. Fastgreedy [**Newman** (2004)], Label_Propagation [**Raghavan et al.** (2007)], Infomap [**Rosvall and Bergstrom** (2008)], Multilevel [**Blondel et al.** (2008)], Walktrap [**Pons and Latapy** (2006)]. In the next section, FSA algorithm is compared with other algorithms, in-terms of modularity and conductance by using LFR benchmark network and varying the mixing parameter μ. The FSA algorithm is also compared with local community detection algorithms, viz., LICOD [**Yakoubi and Kanawati** (2014)], HCLD [**Tabarzad and Hamzeh** (2017)], Local-T [**Fagnan et al.** (2014)], CDERS [**Lim and Datta** (2013)], and ENBC [**Biswas and Biswas** (2015)] using F_score, in section 5.6.

5.2 Evaluation of Proposed Algorithm in terms of Recall and Precision

To calculate precision and recall of the proposed algorithm, following formulations are used:

$$\text{Recall (C)} = \frac{\text{Number of nodes found by the algorithm which belongs to community C}}{\text{Total Number of nodes in the community C}} \quad (5.2.1)$$

$$\text{Precision (C)} = \frac{\text{Number of nodes found by the algorithm which belongs to community C}}{\text{Total number of nodes found by the algorithm}} \quad (5.2.2)$$

The datasets considered to evaluate the proposed algorithm, by calculating recall and precision values of the detected communities, are given below.

5.2.1 Datasets

Zachary's Karate Club network: It is a social network dataset generated by Zachary. The network graph is created by studying the ties among 34 members of a karate club for two years. Due to conflict, the club was divided between two groups [**Zachary** (1977)].

Bottlenose Dolphins network: It is a social network generated by Lusseau [**Lusseau et al.** (2003)] by observing the interaction among 62 Bottlenose Dolphins, throughout seven years in Doubtful Sound, New Zealand.

American Political Book network: This social network dataset is a network of 105 number of political books bought by different Americans from Amazon, created by V. Krebs and divided into groups by Newman [**Krebs** (2017)].

Adjective Noun Network: This network dataset consists of common adjectives and nouns of the novel "David Copperfield" written by Charles Dickens. Here, nodes are the most commonly used adjectives and nouns of the novel; edges are the adjacency of these adjectives and nouns [**Newman** (2006a)].

Relaxed Caveman Network: It is a synthetic network based on Relaxed Caveman [**Watts** (2000)] graph model, consisting of 80 nodes and 8 clusters. Each cluster contains ten nodes with 0.1 being connection probability of each internal node with external nodes.

Chapter 5. *Comparison FSA with other Community Detection Algorithms* 67

Figure 5.1: Books on American Politics Network

Figure 5.2: Adjective Noun Network

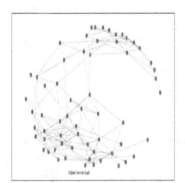

Figure 5.3: Dolphin Network

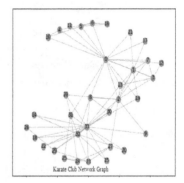

Figure 5.4: Karate Club Network

Planted Partition Network: It is a synthetic shared network of 100 nodes with five communities, based on Planted Partition graph. Here, 25% of the nodes of each community are shared with other communities [**McSherry** (2001)].

The graphical representations of the datasets mentioned above are presented in the Figures 5.1-5.6.

5.2.2 Calculation of Recall and Precision

To calculate precision and recall values, community memberships of all nodes of the networks are required. Predefined memberships of the nodes for Political-Book network and Karate-Club network are referred from [**Newman** (2006b)]. Predefined community memberships for Dolphin network is referred from [**Newman** (2006a)]. Greedy-Modularity

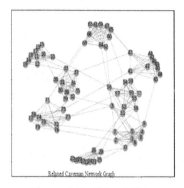

Figure 5.5: Relaxed Caveman Network

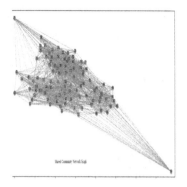

Figure 5.6: Planted-Partition Network

Table 5.1: Recall and Precision values

Network Graph	Recall	SD Recall	Precision	SD Precision
Pol-book network	0.9523	0.0287	0.9736	0.0264
Adj-noun network	0.9822	0.0174	0.9276	0.0477
Dolphin network	0.9735	0.0249	0.9718	0.03944
Karate club network	0.9627	0.04656	0.9219	0.0374
Relaxed Caveman network	1.0	0.0	0.9851	0.0357
Planted-Partition network	0.9857	0.0216	0.9755	0.0370

community detection algorithm [**Newman** (2004)] is employed for obtaining community memberships for Adj-Noun network. The Planted Partition and Relaxed Caveman graphs are artificially generated; hence their community memberships are already known.

Each experiment is conducted for 20 iterations, and the averages values of recall and precision along with their standard deviations (SDs) are tabulated in Table 5.1.

It is depicted from Table 5.1, FSA performs well in recall and precision values. High values of recall and precision (nearer to 1.0) signify that the algorithm can detect communities efficiently. The low values of standard deviation in both recall and precision imply that the algorithm performs uniformly irrespective of the random seed nodes.

5.2.3 Impact of Random Seed Nodes on Recall and Precision

The Local_FSA works with random seed nodes, which are chosen automatically, so it is possible that recall and precision may vary due to distinct seed nodes. Five arbitrary seed nodes from a particular community (for each network) are selected, to study the impact on recall and precision of the detected communities, by executing the Local_FSA. Table

5.2 displays recall, precision and SD values for six different datasets with five distinct seed nodes. The algorithm is implemented locally to discover the communities under study.

Table 5.2: Variations in Recall and Precision

Network	Seed Node	Recall	Precision
Political Book	N28	1.0	0.9783
	N60	1.0	0.9574
	N66	0.9555	0.9555
	N73	0.9555	0.9773
	N84	0.9778	0.9565
SD		0.0199	0.01047
Noun-Adjective Network	N17	1.0	0.8725
	N12	0.9733	0.8488
	N51	.96	0.9605
	N24	0.9733	0.9588
	N25	1.0	0.8795
SD		0.0160	0.0465
Dolphin Network	N18	1.0	1.0
	N58	0.9286	1.0
	N55	1.0	1.0
	N14	1.0	0.9333
	N42	0.9286	0.9286
SD		0.03497	0.03386
Karate Club	N33	1.0	1.0
	N30	1.0	0.9444
	N31	1.0	0.8947
	N27	0.9412	0.9412
	N32	1.0	1.0
SD		0.02352	0.03996
Relaxed Caveman	N1	1.0	1.0
	N2	1.0	1.0
	N3	1.0	0.9
	N4	1.0	1.0
	N5	1.0	1.0
SD		0.0	0.04
Planted Partition Graph	N1	1.0	1.0
	N2	0.95	1.0
	N3	1.0	1.0
	N4	0.95	1.0
	N5	1.0	0.9523
SD		0.0244	0.0190

The standard deviations of recall and precision values are very less. The small variations in the recall and precision signify that, the algorithm is stable irrespective of the selected seed.

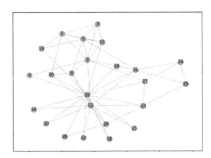

Figure 5.7: Karate-Club network with k=5.0

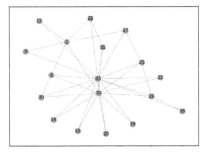

Figure 5.8: Karate-Club network with k=4.5

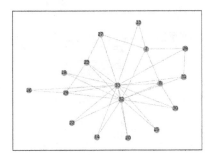

Figure 5.9: Karate-Club network with k=4.0

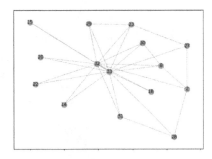

Figure 5.10: Karate-Club network with k=3.5

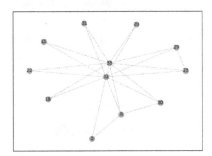

Figure 5.11: Karate-Club network with k=3.0

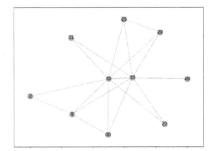

Figure 5.12: Karate-Club network with k=2.5

5.3 Detection of Multiple Resolution Communities with FSA

Average node degree (d) of a network can be defined in terms of the total number of nodes of the community n ($d = n/k$), as described in 4.3.1. Equations 4.3.12 and 4.3.13 suggest that threshold values may be calculated if the value of n and k are known. The FSA is

Chapter 5. Comparison FSA with other Community Detection Algorithms

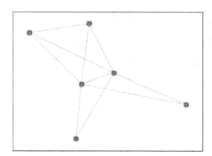

Figure 5.13: Karate-Club network with k=2.0

Table 5.3: Communities with Multiple Resolutions

Value of k	Total number of nodes	Total number of edges
5.0	24	57
4.5	18	37
4.0	17	35
3.5	15	31
3.0	12	23
2.5	10	19
2.0	6	10

flexible enough to find communities of different resolutions, depending upon the value of k. Figures 5.7-5.13 represent multiple resolution community networks with varying values of k from 5.0 to 2.0. Karate Club network is used for this experiment and node 33 is selected as seed. Table 5.3 shows the number of nodes and edges of the discovered communities, with varying values of k. This experiment validates that, the proposed algorithm is efficient in detecting multi-resolution community structures in a network.

5.4 Comparison based on Modularity and Conductance

In this section, the proposed FSA is compared with five different well known, state-of-the-art, community detection algorithms; namely Greedy_modularity [**Newman (2004)**], Label_Propagation [**Raghavan et al. (2007)**], Infomap [**Rosvall and Bergstrom (2008)**], Multilevel [**Blondel et al. (2008)**] and Walktrap [**Pons and Latapy (2006)**]. The algorithms are evaluated using synthetic and real-world networks, in terms of modularity and conductance scores, shown in Tables 5.6-5.7 and Tables 5.8-5.10 respectively.Each of the experiment is conducted for ten iterations, and the maximum, minimum, average scores along with their standard deviations (SDs) are recorded in Tables 5.6-5.10. Since a community with high modularity and low conductance score is considered as a good community, maximum values of modularity and minimum values of conductance are highlighted for convenience.Finally, FSA is compared with a recently proposed GA-based algorithm CC_GA [**Said et al.** (2018)], and the results are presented in Table 5.11.The specifications about the synthetic and real-world networks are given in Table 5.4 and Table 5.5 respectively.

5.4.1 Evaluation of FSA using Synthetic Networks

For Barabasi-Albert preferential attachment and LFR graphs, the proposed algorithm outperforms all the other algorithms used for this experiment, in terms of modularity and conductance scores. Though Label propagation algorithm has better minimum-conductance score than FSA, it performs extremely poor in terms of modularity score (avg modularity for Barbasi graph =0.124591576, avg modularity for LFR graph =0.1145606537). For Relaxed Caveman graph, FSA along with Infomap and Multilevel outperform rest of the algorithms used. For Gaussian Random graph, Multilevel, Greedy modularity, Infomap, and Walktrap algorithms perform best in conductance score, whereas FSA performs better in modularity score. In Newman-Watts-Storagz graph, FSA and Greedy Modularity algorithm detect communities with the best modularity and best conductance scores respectively. In Watts-Storagz graph, FSA scores best in modularity and Multilevel algorithm scores best in conductance.

The proposed FSA has the best modularity scores in most of the networks. The conductance score is better than other algorithms for Planted Partition, LFR and Barabasi-Albert attachment graphs. In other cases, conductance values are close to the best values.

5.4.2 Evaluation of FSA using Real World Networks

As shown in Tables 5.8-5.10, the proposed FSA performs better than other community detection algorithms, in modularity and conductance scores for Collaboration, Political Book, Email, Netsc, PGP, Twitter, Yeast, E. Coli, and American Football networks. In Karate club network, Multilevel algorithm has the best modularity value, whereas, FSA has the best average conductance value and Label Propagation has minimum conductance value. In Dolphin network, FSA is best in modularity score, and Label Propagation is best in conductance score. In Facebook network, Greedy Modularity is better than other algorithms in modularity score. However, the proposed algorithm is better in terms of conductance score. In Jazz network, FSA lags behind Multilevel and Label Propagation algorithms in term of modularity and conductance values respectively.

From the above results, it is concluded that FSA outperforms other community detection algorithms with real-world networks, in terms of modularity and conductance, for most of the cases.

Chapter 5. *Comparison FSA with other Community Detection Algorithms* 73

Table 5.4: Specifications of Synthetic Networks

Network	Specifications
Barabasi Albert preferential attachment graph [**Barabási and Albert** (1999)]	1000 nodes and 11856 edges
Relaxed Caveman Graph [**Watts** (2000)]	1000 nodes, 50 clusters of size 20 each, probability of linking to different clusters = 0.3
Gaussian Random Partition Graph	1500 nodes, 30 mean cluster size, probability of intra-cluster connection= 0.5, probability of inter-cluster connection = 0.05
LFR Benchmark Graph [**Lancichinetti and Fortunato** (2009)]	2500 nodes, power law exponent of the degree=3.0, power law exponent of the community size=1.5, average degree of nodes=10, minimum community size=25, inter-community edges incident to each node = 0.25
Newman Watts Strogatz Graph [**Newman et al.** (2001)]	1000 nodes, each node joined with 20 neighbors
Planted Partition Graph [**McSherry** (2001)]	1000 nodes with 50 groups, probability of connecting inside= 0.5, probability of connecting to outside=0.05
Watts Strogatz Graphn [**Watts and Strogatz** (1998)]	1000 nodes, each node joined with 20 neighbors

Table 5.5: Specifications of Real-World Networks

Network	Specifications
Collaboration [Watts (2000)]	Co-authorship of published articles in arXiv in the area of relativity and quantum cosmology. 5242 nodes(scientists) 14,446 edges(collaborations).
Email [Leskovec and Krevl (2014)]	Email between members of European Research Institute. 1005 nodes(members), 16706 edges(Email).
Karate Club [Zachary (1977)]	Zachary's Karate club network. 34 nodes(members) and 78 edges(interactions).
Netsc [Newman (2006a)]	Co-authorship network of scientists in the field of network science. 1589 nodes(scientists), 2741 edges(co-authorship).
PGP [Boguná et al. (2004)]	Web-trust network of signature for private communication. 10680 nodes (web users), 24316 edges (bi-directional signatures).
Twitter [Leskovec and Mcauley (2012)]	Online Social Network. 23370 nodes(users), 32831 edges(followings).
Yeast [Kim et al. (2014)]	A probabilistic functional gene network for Baker's yeast. 4172 nodes(genes) and 81953 edges (relations).
Ecoli Shen-Orr et al. (2002)	Biological transcriptional regulatory network. 418 nodes(genes) and 519 edges (regulatory links).
Dolphin [Lusseau et al. (2003)]	Bottlenose dolphin social network by Lusseau. 62 nodes(Dolphins) and 159 edges(interactions).
Facebook [Leskovec and Mcauley (2012)]	Online social network. 2888 nodes(users) and 2981 edges(friendship).
Football [Evans (2012)]	American college football network. 115 nodes(teams)and 613 edges (matches).
Jazz [Gleiser and Danon (2003)]	Collaborative network of musicians. 198 nodes(musicians) and 5484 edges(collaborations).
Pol. Book [Krebs (2017)]	Network of political books bought by Americans. 105 nodes(books) and 441 (co-purchase).

Table 5.6: Modularity and Conductance Values for Synthetic Networks

Graph	Algorithm	Modularity				Conductance			
		Avg	Max	Min	SD	Avg	Max	Min	SD
Barbasi-Albert	Proposed	**0.462217475**	**0.46226524**	0.46218886	2.49111E-05	**0.3755229236**	0.37558914	**0.37548263**	3.46052E-05
	Multilevel	0.43783840	0.43783840	0.43783840	0.0	0.39638362	0.39638362	0.39638362	0.0
	Label Prop	0.1245591576	0.36604539	0.0	0.09767712	0.67299444	1.0	**0.24550898**	0.23360948
	Infomap	0.43570517	0.44210745	0.42887078	0.0037652544	0.4531048	0.46385399	0.44077122	0.00658332
	Greedy Mod.	0.41679248	0.41679248	0.41679248	0.0	0.4321058	0.43210580	0.4321058	0.0
	Walktrap	0.36870054	0.36870054	0.36870054	0.0	0.45056751	0.45056751	0.45056751	0.0
Relaxed Caveman	Proposed	**0.64645232**	**0.64645232**	0.64645232	0.0	**0.25407261**	0.25407261	**0.25407261**	0.0
	Multilevel	**0.64645432**	**0.64645432**	0.64645432	0.0	**0.2640726**	0.2540726	0.2540726	0.0
	Label Prop	0.6453669	**0.64645432**	0.63558024	0.0034386841	0.25546663	0.2640726	0.25801293	0.0019162368
	Infomap	**0.64645432**	**0.64645432**	0.64645432	0.0	**0.2540726**	0.2540726	**0.2540726**	0.0
	Greedy Mod	0.60025925	0.60025925	0.60025925	0.0	0.2705183	0.2705183	0.2705183	0.0
	Walktrap	0.64156049	0.64156049	0.64156049	0.0	0.2570058	0.2570058	0.2570058	0.0
Gaussian Random	proposed	**0.36270018**	**0.36270018**	0.36270018	0.0	0.13736295	0.13736295	0.13736295	0.0
	Multilevel	0.35497142	0.35497142	0.35497142	0.0	**0.128508012**	0.12850812	**0.12850812**	0.0
	Label Prop	0.31947427	0.35497141	0.0	0.11225181	0.21565731	1.0	**0.12850812**	0.27558992
	Infomap	0.35497141	0.35497141	0.35497141	0.0	**0.12850812**	0.12850812	**0.12850812**	0.0
	Greedy Mod	0.35497141	0.35497141	0.35497141	0.0	**0.12850812**	0.12850812	**0.12850812**	0.0
	Walktrap	0.35497141	0.35497141	0.35497141	0.0	**0.12850812**	0.12850812	**0.12850812**	0.0
LFR	Proposed	**0.4219240071**	**0.42198445**	0.42180986	4.54103E-05	**0.3911426709**	0.39148834	**0.391133682**	4.5042E-05
	Multilevel	0.41581204	0.41581204	0.415812049557	0.0	0.39970851	0.399708518	0.39970851	0.0
	Label Prob	0.1145606537	0.323916494	0.0135211158	0.0932873074	**0.024444444**	0.24444444	**0.0**	0.077300120
	Infomap	0.39038007	0.39671341	0.386966813	0.0031059893	0.48545871	0.490155172	0.47628866	0.0042811215
	Greedy Mod	0.41730976	0.41730976	0.41730976	0.0	0.40157066	0.40157066	0.40157066	0.0
	Walktrap	0.34132427	0.34132427	0.34132427	0.0	0.46834257	0.46834257	0.468342579	0.0

Table 5.7: Modularity and Conductance Values for Synthetic Networks (In continuation of Table 5.6)

Graph	Algorithm	Modularity				Conductance			
		Avg	Max	Min	SD	Avg	Max	Min	SD
Newman-Watts	Proposed	**0.611236177**	**0.61238903**	0.61232487	2.08904E-05	0.226945372	0.22698582	0.22689334	3.38938E-05
	Multilevel	0.50962641	0.509626641	0.50962641	0.0	0.1570302	0.1570302	0.1570302	0.0
	Label Prop	0.559655098	0.57352826	0.5412653	0.0110314	0.30658392	0.36122414	0.25771604	0.030233499
	Infomap	0.59404136	0.59427986	0.593038735	0.00050280581	0.239550963	0.24095096	0.2391493	0.00075964378
	Greedy Mod	0.51179638	0.51179638	0.51179638	0.0	**0.14811205**	0.14811205	**0.14811205**	0.0
	Walktrap	0.59005721	0.59005721	0.59005721	0.0	0.24449893	0.24449893	0.24449893	0.0
Planted Partition	Proposed	**0.41214592**	**0.41214592**	0.41214592	0.0	**0.45721654**	0.45721654	**0.45721654**	0.0
	Multilevel	0.38425449	0.38425449	0.38425449	0.0	0.471130349	0.47130349	0.47130349	0.0
	Label Prop	0.10559975	0.39540598	0.0	0.17270796	0.831168483	1.0	**0.35559787**	0.27312732
	Infomap	0.39479953	0.39479953	0.39479953	0.0	0.5048392	0.5048392	0.5048392	0.0
	Greedy Mod	0.3636132	0.3636132	0.3636132	0.0	0.46820733	0.46820733	0.46820733	0.0
	Walktrap	0.37840099	0.37840099	0.37840099	0.0	0.54384223	0.54384223	0.54384223	0.0
Watts Strogatz	Proposed	**0.60113207**	**0.60113207**	0.60113207	0.0	0.19212054	0.19212054	0.19212054	0.0
	Multilevel	0.526422	0.526422	0.526422	0.0	**0.13922874**	0.13922874	**0.13922874**	0.0
	Label Prop	0.56768	0.583506	0.555164	0.008253032	0.3095087	0.348881294	0.21813222	0.03978779
	Infomap	0.5872176	0.59169	0.583054	0.00388175	0.28644184	0.30077488	0.26896316	0.014632371
	Greedy Mod	0.512438	0.512438	0.512438	0.0	0.15350386	0.15350386	0.15350386	0.0
	Walktrap	0.597704	0.597704	0.597704	0.0	0.23463699	0.23463699	0.23463699	0.0

Table 5.8: Modularity and Conductance Values for Real-World Networks

Graph	Algorithm	Modularity				Conductance			
		Avg	Max	Min	SD	Avg	Max	Min	SD
Collaboration	Proposed	**0.86153846**	**0.86153846**	0.86153846	0.0	**0.01068552**	0.01068552	**0.01068552**	0.0
	Multilevel	0.84125015	0.84125015	0.84125015	0.0	0.120707149	0.120707149	0.120707149	0.0
	Label Prop	0.794458988	0.8018414	0.79067722	0.003756012	0.13178136	0.13706353	0.12713332	0.00274261
	Infomap	0.794335193	0.796672198	0.79194442	0.00147729	0.12614283	0.12873627	0.12210227	0.00230815
	Greedy Mod	0.8045631	0.8045631	0.8045631	0.0	0.018230676	0.018230067	0.018230067	0.0
	Walktrap	0.78248973	0.78248973	0.78248973	0.0	0.15837981	0.15837981	0.15837981	0.0
Email	Proposed	**0.423251954**	**0.42327711**	0.42322772	1.54317E-05	**0.118939345**	0.11896931	**0.11890783**	1.99533E-05
	Multilevel	0.41118306	0.41118306	0.41118306	0.0	0.12741015	0.12741015	0.12741015	0.0
	Label Prop	0.012974294	0.090544014	0.0043025283	0.027255343	0.16337917	0.17649132	0.1583156	0.00697845
	Infomap	0.41651083	0.41695809	0.41614326	0.000336579	0.29705997	0.30060884	0.28796483	0.0039894459
	Greedy Mod	0.365244402	0.365244402	0.365244402	0.0	0.2516535	0.2516535	0.2516535	0.0
	Walktrap	0.371190585	0.371190585	0.371190585	0.0	0.691162533	0.691162533	0.691162533	0.0
Karate Club	Proposed	0.40836217	0.40836217	0.40836217	0.0	**0.196252285**	0.19625285	0.19625285	0.0
	Multilevel	**0.41880341**	**0.41880341**	0.41880341	0.0	0.28793309	0.28793309	0.28793309	0.0
	Label Prop	0.350386625	0.41510519	0.0	0.1242051	0.2619684	1.0	**0.128205128205**	0.264360927103
	Infomap	0.40203813	0.40203813	0.40203813	0.0	0.201133719	0.201133719	0.201133719	0.0
	Greedy Mod	0.3806706	0.3806706	0.3806706	0.0	0.2808302	0.2808302	0.2808302	0.0
	Walktrap	0.3532215	0.3532215	0.3532215	0.0	0.40809523	0.40809523	0.40809523	0.0
Netsc	Proposed	**0.9585509905**	**0.95854258**	0.95848811	1.76644E-05	**0.300718662**	.30074131	**0.30070856**	8.7623E-06
	Multilevel	0.9577347	0.9577347	0.9577347	0.0	0.31621021	0.31621021	0.31621021	0.0
	Label Prop	0.909254877	0.92015184	0.89764481	0.00673972	0.30945147	0.31130499	0.30793506	0.00122439
	Infomap	0.929332669	0.93031907	0.92896023	0.00059732	0.305508458	0.305515111	0.30493696	8.3564874e-05
	Greedy Mod	0.929332669	0.93031907	0.92896023	0.00059732	0.305508458	0.305515111	0.30493696	8.3564874e-05
	Walktrap	0.95597277	0.95597277	0.95597277	0.0	0.31148403	0.31148403	0.31148403	0.0

Table 5.9: Modularity and Conductance Values for Real-World Networks (In continuation of Table 5.8)

Graph	Algorithm	Modularity				Conductance			
		Avg	Max	Min	SD	Avg	Max	Min	SD
PGP	Proposed	**0.87170003**	**0.87170003**	0.87170003	0.0	**0.06537782**	0.06537782	**0.06537782**	0.0
	Multilevel	0.859587754	0.859587754	0.859587754	0.0	0.09262664	0.09262664	0.09262664	0.0
	Label Prop	0.8055388	0.8192046	0.7924703	0.0076508	0.18245328	0.18632097	0.17742624	0.00257085
	Infomap	0.80123501	0.80216304	0.799274435	0.00100482	0.1914648	0.192221963	0.190083542	0.00062013
	Greedy Mod	0.856452907	0.856452907	0.856452907	0.0	0.07271419	0.07271419	0.07271419	0.0
	Walktrap	0.7894202	0.7894202	0.7894202	0.0	0.24025269	0.24025269	0.24025269	0.0
Twitter	Proposed	**0.89661855**	**0.89661855**	0.89661855	0.0	**0.038835619**	0.038835619	**0.038835619**	0.0
	Multilevel	0.866236551	0.866236551	0.866236551	0.0	0.03974205	0.03974205	0.03974205	0.0
	Label Prop	0.793293543	0.802155134	0.78320292	0.00528305	0.19536893	0.20476605	0.18738220	0.00602302
	Infomap	0.82524101	0.82687861	0.824311713	0.00085536	0.18135357	0.182543362	0.17900480	0.00100699
	Greedy Mod	0.86934555	0.86934555	0.86934555	0.0	0.04250495	0.04250495	0.04250495	0.0
	Walktrap	0.85228512	0.85228512	0.85228512	0.0	0.10677522	0.10677522	0.10677522	0.0
Yeast	Proposed	**0.681658361**	**0.681669555**	0.68164109	7.8005E-06	**0.084592892**	0.08459804	**0.084586255**	4.34955E-06
	Multilevel	0.66022337	0.66022337	0.66022337	0.0	0.1308817534,	0.1308817534	0.1308817534	0.0
	Label Prop	0.61876314	0.63140643	0.593371545	0.01296553	0.272611272	0.29847784	0.24452698	0.02179358
	Infomap	0.62036554	0.62117961	0.6193235	0.000576629	0.36609700	0.370505735	0.36670922	0.00317259
	Greedy Mod	0.57000291	0.57000291	0.57000291	0.0	0.14736525	0.14736525	0.14736525	0.0
	Walktrap	0.63951646	0.63951646	0.63951646	0.0	0.44274368,	0.44274368	0.44274368	0.0
Ecoli	Proposed	**0.78741415**	**0.78741415**	0.78741415	0.0	**0.15643401**	0.15643401	**0.15643401**	0.0
	Multilevel	0.77965051	0.77965051	0.77965051	0.0	0.16225618	0.16225618	0.16225618	0.0
	Label Prop	0.74131786	0.76550480	0.71137573	0.01577472,	0.18266417	0.223331145	0.156653098	0.01985117
	Infomap	0.73099907	0.73184171	0.73063794	0.00058147	0.25090761	0.253377492	0.24967876	0.00197863
	Greedy Mod	0.77841261	0.77841261	0.77841261	0.0	0.162127781372;	0.16212778	0.16212778	0.0
	Walktrap	0.74629400	0.74629400	0.74629400	0.0	0.17055694	0.17055694	0.17055694	0.0

Table 5.10: Modularity and Conductance Values for Real-World Networks (In continuation of Table 5.8)

Graph	Algorithm	Modularity				Conductance			
		Avg	Max	Min	SD	Avg	Max	Min	SD
Dolphin	Proposed	**0.528739932**	**0.528739932**	0.528739332	0.0	0.29153396	0.29153396	0.29153396	0.0
	Multilevel	0.51853170	0.51853170	0.51853170,	0.0	0.39074555	0.39074555	0.39074555	0.0
	Label Prop	0.500077713	0.518571250	0.44806376	0.023267725	0.242999873	0.26699443	**0.221832553**	0.017863097
	Infomap	0.526011558	0.52851944	0.52474190	0.00166010,	0.429811754	0.44135972	0.41118004	0.01497914
	Greedy Mod	0.49549068	0.49549068	0.49549068	0.0	0.453305459	0.45305459	0.453305459	0.0
	Walktrap	0.48884537	0.48884537	0.48884537	0.0	0.40507067	0.40507067	0.40507067	0.0
Facebook	Proposed	0.80745637	0.80745637	0.80745637	0.0	**0.081333839**	0.08133839	**0.081333839**	0.0
	Multilevel	0.8086875	0.8086875	0.8086875	0.0	0.12179438	0.12179438	0.12179438	0.0
	Label Prop	0.795116083	0.79991928	0.79426049	0.0016838239	0.163434325	0.167284267	0.141051065	0.0078959995
	Infomap	0.796123357	0.796123357	0.796123357	0.0	0.21754008	0.21754008	0.21754008	0.0
	Greedy Mod	**0.808721775**	**0.808721775**	0.808721775	0.0	0.12179826	0.12179826	0.12179826	0.0
	Walktrap	0.63305553	0.63305553	0.63305553	0.0	0.17201910	0.17201910	0.17201910	0.0
American Football	Proposed	**0.607705324**	**0.607705324**	0.60705324	0.0	**0.29214832**	0.29214832	0.29214832	0.0
	Multilevel	0.604566956	0.604566956	0.604566956	0.0	0.29409958	0.29409958	0.29409958	0.0
	Label Prop	0.589168994	0.60320436	0.55335857	0.014861276	0.32487178	0.36581379	**0.273886174**	0.030230078
	Infomap	0.600516154	0.600516154	0.600516154	0.0	0.337182910	0.337182910	0.337182910	0.0
	Greedy Mod	0.54974066	0.54974066	0.549740660	0.0	0.29787056	0.29787056	0.29787056	0.0
	Walktrap	0.602914290	0.602914290	0.60291429	0.0	0.29414871	0.29414871	0.29414871	0.0
Jazz	Proposed	0.440678710	0.440678710	0.44067871	0.0	0.45786563	0.45786563	0.45786563	0.0
	Multilevel	**0.445144384**	**0.445144384**	0.44514384	0.0	0.454086200	0.45408620	0.45408620	0.0
	Label Prop	0.30390432	0.44277358	0.0	0.12839680	**0.257555156**	1.0	**0.125**	0.26345458
	Infomap	0.280000040	0.280000040	0.280000400	0.0	0.542100065	0.542100065	0.542100065	0.0
	Greedy Mod	0.43890781	0.43890781	0.43890781	0.0	0.49308714	0.49308714	0.49308714	0.0
	Walktrap	0.43842148	0.43842148	0.43842148	0.0	0.70948610	0.70948610	0.70948610	0.0
Political Book	Proposed	**0.524469105**	**0.524469105**	0.52469105	0.0	**0.205006871**	0.20506871	0.20506871	0.0
	Multilevel	0.520048529	0.520048529	0.52048529	0.0	0.205144330	0.20514433	0.20514433	0.0
	Label Prop	0.499628490	0.522228101	0.488500160	0.01021176	0.187574110	0.36483251	**0.119593338**	0.08163863
	Infomap	0.522847990	0.522847990	0.522847990	0.0	0.280065070	0.28006507	0.28006507	0.0
	Greedy Mod	0.501974480	0.501974480	0.501974480	0.0	0.254911440,	0.25491144	0.25491144	0.0
	Walktrap	0.506972400	0.506972400	0.50697240	0.0	0.206519440	0.20651944	0.20651944	0.0

Table 5.11: Compariosn Between CC_GA and FSA Based on Modularity

Graph	CC_GA			Proposed FSA		
	Max	Avg	SD	Max	Avg	SD
Karate	**0.42**	**0.42**	0.0	0.40836217	0.40836217	0.0
Dolphin	**0.529**	526	0.003	0.52873932	**0.52873932**	0.0
American Football	0.594	563	0.020	**0.60705324**	**0.60705324**	0.0
Political Book	**0.527**	**0.525**	0.002	0.52469105	0.52469105	0.0
E. Coli	0.786	0.778	0.005	**0.78741415**	**0.78741415**	0.0
Netsc	0.958	0.955	0.002	**0.95854258**	**0.958509905**	1.76644E-05
Facebook	**0.809**	**0.809**	0.0	0.80745637	0.80745637	0.0
Collab	0.828	0.821	0.004	**0.86153846**	**0.86153846**	0.0
PGP	0.852	843	0.005	**0.87170003**	**0.87170003**	0.0
Twitter	0.864	0.862	0.002	**0.89661855**	**0.89661855**	0.0
Jazz	**0.444**	0.437	0.008	0.44067871	**0.44067871**	0.0

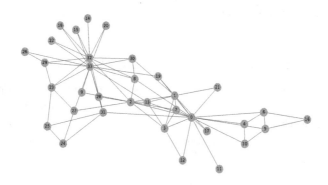

Figure 5.14: The Karate Club network

5.4.3 Comparison of FSA with Genetic Algorithm Based Algorithm

The proposed FSA is compared with CC_GA(a GA based algorithm [**Said et al.** (2018)]), based on the modularity score, as presented in Table 5.11. FSA has better modularity scores for American Football, Dolphin, E.Coli, Netsc, Collaboration, PGP and Twitter networks; whereas CC_GA has better modularity scores for Karate Club, Political Book networks. CC_GA is better in maximum-modularity score for Dolphin and Jazz networks. However, FSA is better than CC_GA in average-modularity scores.

Chapter 5. Comparison FSA with other Community Detection Algorithms

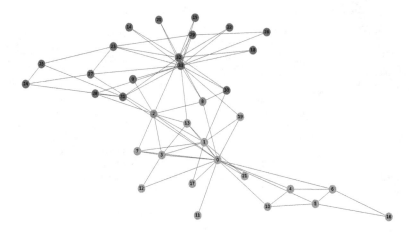

Figure 5.15: The Karate Club network with overlapping communities(Nodes 2 and 8 are shared between both communities).

5.5 Comparison with LFR Benchmark Networks

LFR benchmark synthetic network is a randomly generated network with a predefined community structure. The mixing parameter (μ) in LFR is used to control the overlapping between communities. The value of μ ranges from 0.1 to 1.0 for the experiments. When the value of μ is greater than 0.5, the generated network's community structure becomes highly distorted.

In this experiment, Multilevel, Label Propagation, Infomap, Fastgreedy, Walktrap, and the proposed FSA community detection algorithms are evaluated using LFR benchmark networks with varying mixing parameter values. There are two sets of networks. The first set of networks have 1000 nodes with power-law exponent for degree distribution is 2.5, power-law exponent for community size distribution is 1.5, average node degree is 20, maximum node degree is 50, size of communities are ranging from 25 to 50. Ten different networks of similar configurations are generated by varying the value of μ from 0.1 to 1.0.

The second set of networks have 5000 nodes with power-law exponent for degree distribution is 2.5, power-law exponent for community size distribution is 1.5, average node degree is 20, maximum node degree is 50, the minimum size of the community is 25, the maximum size of the community is 100. The value of μ is varied between 0.1 to 1.0 to create 10 such networks.

Table 5.12: Predefined Community structure for local community detection

Network	nodes	edges	communities	descriptions
Karate club	34	78	2	Social network of karate club members
Dolphin	62	159	2	Interaction network of Bottlenose dolphins
Political books	105	441	3	Network of political books bought from Amazon on American politics
LFR	1000	15070	152	Synthetic network with minimum node degree 30, average node degree 100, minimum community size 40, maximum community size 100, mixing parameter is 0.1

The comparison of modularity and conductance values for all the evaluated algorithms on the two sets of networks (1000 and 5000 nodes) are shown in Figures 5.14 and 5.15, respectively.

Across all the synthetic networks, the modularity value decreases, and the conductance value increases with the increase in the mixing parameter μ. As shown in Figure 5.14, FSA, Multilevel, Fastgreedy, and Walktrap have similar performance for modularity and conductance. However, the performance of Label propagation and Infomap degrades rapidly for mixing parameter values greater than 0.5. Also, it can be noticed from Figure 5.15, FSA, Multilevel, Fastgreedy algorithms perform similarly, while Label propagation, Infomap algorithms perform poorly both in-terms of modularity and conductance for mixing parameter values greater than 0.6.

In all the LFR benchmark networks, the proposed FSA performs reasonably and competitively.

5.6 Comparison for Local Community Detection Algorithms

In this section, FSA is compared with other local community detection algorithms, namely, LICOD [**Yakoubi and Kanawati** (2014)], HCLD [**Tabarzad and Hamzeh** (2017)], Local-T [**Fagnan et al.** (2014)], CDERS [**Lim and Datta** (2013)], and ENBC [**Biswas and Biswas** (2015)]. The experiments are conducted with ground-truth networks having predefined community membership. F_measure accuracy is used for the evaluation, described by the equation given below.

$$F_{measure} = \frac{2 * precision * recall}{precision + recall} \quad (5.6.1)$$

The descriptions of the data sets used for the experiments are given in Table 5.12.

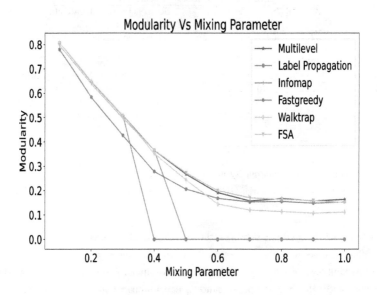
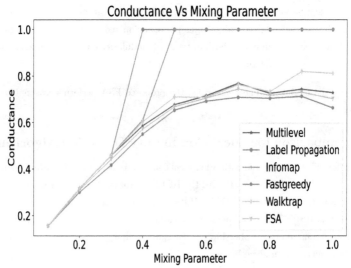

Figure 5.16: Modularity and Conductance for LFR network with 1000 nodes and Mixing parameter μ varies from 0.1 to 1.0.

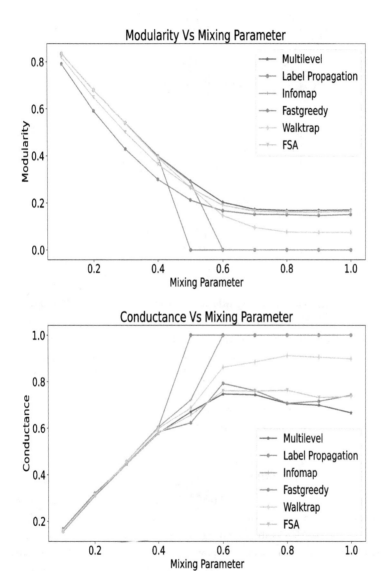

Figure 5.17: Modularity and Conductance LFR network with 5000 nodes and Mixing parameter μ varies from 0.1 to 1.0.

Table 5.13: Comparison for local community detection, $F_{measure}$

network	algorithm	$F_{measure}$
Karate club	Proposed FSA	**0.9513**
	LICOD	0.8824
	HCLD	0.9394
	Local-T	0.9394
	CDERS	0.8318
	ENBC	0.9394
Bottlenose dolphin	Proposed FSA	0.8825
	LICOD	0.4719
	HCLD	**0.8896**
	Local-T	0.6045
	CDERS	**0.8896**
	ENBC	0.6707
Political book	Proposed FSA	**0.9016**
	LICOD	0.8143
	HCLD	0.8835
	Local-T	0.8702
	CDERS	0.8315
	ENBC	0.8702
LFR	Proposed FSA	**1.0**
	LICOD	0.9957
	HCLD	**1.0**
	Local-T	0.5040
	CDERS	0.9127
	ENBC	0.9976

The $F_{measure}$ values of the algorithms are presented in Table 5.13 [**Tabarzad and Hamzeh** (2017)]. In Karate club network, the proposed FSA algorithm performs best with $F_{measure}$ 0.9513. In Bottlenose dolphin network, HCLD and CDERS algorithms perform best with $F_{measure}$ 0.8896. However, FSA performs second best with $F_{measure}$ 0.8825. LICOD performs worst with $F_{measure}$ 0.4719. The best value of $F_{measure}$ is 0.9016 for FSA with Political book network. For LFR network, both FSA and HCLD perform best with $F_{measure}$ 1.0, while Local-T has worst performance with $F_{measure}$ 0.5040. FSA has best $F_{measure}$ across all the ground-truth networks except in Bottlnose dolphin network, where it has second best result.

5.7 Chapter Summary

High values of precision and recall are obtained for the detected communities, discovered by employing FSA with some well known social networks. The proposed algorithm can work both at the local level with a specific seed node, and at network level by automatically selecting random seed nodes. The proposed algorithm performs efficiently even in the presence of shared communities. By controlling the threshold value, the proposed Fire Spread algorithm detects multiple-resolution hierarchical community structures. The FSA does not require a predefined value for the total number of communities of a network. The algorithm is executed locally with distinct seed nodes and is found to be capable of finding similar communities with little variance. The proposed Fire Spread algorithm outperformed some of the well-known algorithms, in terms of conductance and modularity, for which community detection is conducted on various synthetic and real-world networks. The proposed algorithm is also evaluated using the LFR benchmark networks. Finally, the algorithm is compared with other local community detection algorithms based on $F_{measure}$ using networks with predefined community structure. From the results, it can be concluded that the performance of FSA is superior for several networks and competitive for all of the networks used in the evaluation.

Chapter 6
EFFECT OF VARYING COMMUNITY STRUCTURE ON NETWORK

6.1 Outline

In this chapter the effects of community formation is uncovered by varying the community structure of the networks. Planted partition networks and Relaxed caveman networks are used for the study. The community structure of these synthetic networks are varied and the effect on these networks are analyzed. A detailed analysis of the effect of community formation on the network structure, on average shortest path length (APL) of the network in particular, is conducted which would help quantify the effect of community structure on the network. Social networks have lesser diameters and have shorter average path lengths between the participant nodes due to preferential attachment and community structures, as explained by the authors [**Barabási and Albert** (1999)] . Though it is a common belief that community structures contribute to shorter average path lengths [**Sallaberry et al.**

(2013)], by experimenting we found that the grouping of nodes (community structure) in social networks results in lengthening of the APLs between the participating nodes. A random graph is found to have a lesser APL than a social network with community structure. As the size of individual communities increases, there is a decrease in the difference of average shortest path lengths, compared with a random graph containing equal nodes and edges. This relationship is used to predict the average community size and their numbers in a network. The findings mentioned above are applied for the performance enhancement of the proposed FSA algorithm and named as Enhanced Fire Spread community detection algorithm (EFSA).

The organization of this chapter is as follows. In Section 6.2, an efficient and faster method is proposed to find the APL of the Erdos-Renyi random graph using probabilistic method. The proposed method is used in our work to calculated the APLs. In section 6.3, the relation between community structure and APL is investigated. In section 6.4, the effect of mean size of communities and node degree on APL is analyzed. The path length between any two community member nodes is predicted in section 6.5. In the next section, a novel community detection algorithm is proposed and evaluated by comparing it with some of the state of the art community discovery algorithms. The findings and equations obtained from previous sections are used for the proposed enhancement of the FSA algorithm.

6.2 Algorithm to Find APL of a Random Graph

In this section, an algorithm is proposed to predict the APL of a random Erdos-Renyi graph having N nodes and E edges, without constructing the graph and calculating the distance between each pair of nodes. To use the APLs of the Erdos-Renyi graph, reading from one graph is not enough. We need to create l number of Erdos-Renyi graphs, each having N nodes and E edges, and take an average. However, the proposed algorithm, discussed here, is a straightforward method to approximate APLs using probabilistic methods. Though the classical approximation methods like Breadth-first sampling (BFS) can reduce the time required to get the APL of a network, the method's efficiency is highly dependent on the initial node and prone to inaccurate estimations [**Matsumura et al.** (2018)].

The average node degree d of a random graph having N nodes and E edges is calculated as $d = (2 * E)/N$. Therefore, each node of the graph can link to d other nodes with direct-links, on average (from $N-1$ available nodes as self-edges are not allowed). To calculate the APL, we start with a source node; probabilistically compute its distance to all the other nodes (expected distance between the source node to any other node of the graph). All the nodes are assumed to have same degrees to simplify the calculations. The

Chapter 6. *Effect of Varying Community Structure on Network*

number of nodes at a $1-edge$ distance (neighbor nodes) is estimated initially. Similarly, number of nodes at $2-edge, 3-edge, ...R-edge$ ($1 <= R < N$) distances are estimated and the APL is calculated.

6.2.1 Nodes at 1-Edge Distance from Source

It is assumed that each node is linked to d other nodes of the graph. Therefore, the source will have d paths having $1-edge$ distance (on average). Each of these d nodes will connect to $d-1$ other nodes (one link is already used to connect to the source node). d nodes at $1-edge$ distance are expected to connect with $d*(d-1)$ other nodes with edges. However, not all the $d*(d-1)$ edges connect to distinct new nodes, which means some of the edges are from the d nodes at $1-edge$ distance from the source. In that case, fewer than $d*(d-1)$ nodes have $2-edge$ distance from the source.

6.2.2 Number of Nodes at R-Edge Distance from Source Node

Let T be the number of nodes which already have d connections, and they won't participate in any new connections, t be the number nodes at $(R-1)$-edge distance (for any integer value of $R < N$) from source. After the source node is connected to d neighboring nodes, the value of T becomes 1 and value of t becomes d. Let A be the number of distinct nodes that are already connected with the source node at a distance R. For any specific node among the t nodes; the node can connect to 1 new node and $d-1$ old nodes (nodes that are already connected to source) or 2 new nodes and $d-2$ old nodes and so on. The number of occurrences that any node is connected with k new nodes and $d-k$ old nodes, is given by Equation 6.2.1.

$$\binom{t+A}{d-k} \times \binom{N-T-t-A-1}{k} \qquad (6.2.1)$$

where $t+A$ is possible number of old nodes (nodes which already have paths to the source node), $N-T-t-A-1$ are possible number of new nodes (N-1 is considered in place of N since source is not considered, and $A =$ new nodes already connected with source node at a distance R).

The total number of possible occurrences of edges for a node, not yet connected with other nodes, is given in equation 6.2.2:

$$\binom{N-T-1}{d} \qquad (6.2.2)$$

where $N-T-1$ is the possible number of nodes to connect, and d is the total edges of the specific node. Therefore, the probability of any specific node n, connected to k new

```
avg_shortest_path_len_random(N, E):
Data : Total nodes=N, Total edges=E
Result: APL
d = 2 × E/n
t = d
T = 0
s = d
while i ranges from 2 to N-1 do
    if (N − T − 1) ≤ (1) then
     |  break
    else
     |  A=0
    end
    while j in range 1 to t do
        while k in range 1 to d do
         |  A = A + k × ((t+A choose d-k) × (N-T-t-A-1 choose k))/(N-T-1 choose d)
        end
    end
    T = T + t
    t = A
    s = s + i × t
end
return s/(N − 1)
```

Algorithm 5: APL of a Random Graph

nodes and $d - k$ old nodes is given by equation 6.2.3:

$$\frac{\binom{t+A}{d-k} \times \binom{N-T-t-A-1}{k}}{\binom{N-T-1}{d}} \tag{6.2.3}$$

Now, the expected number of new nodes connected by node n is given by equation 6.2.4:

$$k \times \frac{\binom{t+A}{d-k} \times \binom{N-T-t-A-1}{k}}{\binom{N-T-1}{d}} \tag{6.2.4}$$

where the value of k ranges from 1 to d.

Updated A value is written as:

$$A_{new} = A_{old} + k \times \frac{\binom{t+A}{d-k} \times \binom{N-T-t-A-1}{k}}{\binom{N-T-1}{d}} \tag{6.2.5}$$

$T + t$ is updated as the value of T and value of t is updated as $t = A$.

Chapter 6. *Effect of Varying Community Structure on Network* 91

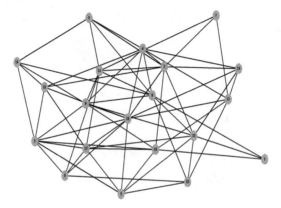

Figure 6.1: A Erdos-Renyi random graph with 20 nodes and 65 edges.

An example

The algorithm is explained with an example. Given above Figure 6.1 is a Erdos-Renyi random network with 20 nodes and 65 edges. The average degree is 6.5. The value of d converted to nearest integer is 6. The value of t, which signifies the number of links at distance R ($R = 1$ here) from the source, is initialized to 6. Value of T, which signifies the number of nodes (except source) already have d links and won't participate in any new link, is initialized to zero. Value of s, which signifies cumulative distance of source from connected nodes that are at 1-edge distance, is set to $s = 6$. For $R = 2$; $t = 10.5849$, $T = 6$, and $s = 27.1699$. For $R = 3$; $t = 1.5723$, $T = 16.5849$, and $s = 31.8870$. For $R = 4$; $t = 0$, $T = 18.157327769833987$ and $s = 31.8870$. As the value of t becomes 0, the algorithm stops. Now, the APL is calculated as $s/19 = 1.6782$. The APL calculated using Dijkstra's algorithm is 1.6844. The error percentage is 0.36764. Though the values of t and T are integer values, the values may take fractional values during the execution of the algorithm.

For the evaluation of the proposed method to calculate average path length of the network, ten random graphs using Erdos-Renyi graph model are constructed, and the shortest path lengths for all these graphs are computed using all pairs shortest path algorithm. Each of the experiment is iterated for ten executions, and the average values are considered. The obtained results are then compared with the average shortest path lengths, calculated using the proposed algorithm. The results are presented in Table 6.1. The average path lengths calculated using the proposed algorithm are approximately similar to the average path lengths computed using all-pair shortest algorithm. The maximum

Table 6.1: Average Shortest Path Lengths Predicted using the Proposed Algorithm

Number of Nodes	Number of Edges	Value by Proposed Algo	Value by Shortest Path Algo	Difference in Percentage
180	450	3.43827893066	3.41070763501	0.80837464244%
256	797	3.41230660897	3.40924500948	0.0898028590231%
270	958	3.13562033093	3.06965244586	2.14903433626%
270	1080	2.92639586744	2.90918697508	0.591536140803%
400	1692	3.009983568543	3.03717766639	0.8953739568131027%
396	1867	2.942001015642	2.90214550569	1.3733119126473323%
396	2017	2.84771533648	2.8190346503	1.01739388601%
403	2227	2.75127960388	2.74879325457	0.0904523941597%
392	2272	2.7456650088615	2.69716060337	1.7983506592412553%
405	2532	2.64899156582	2.64899156582	0.3117243356508649%

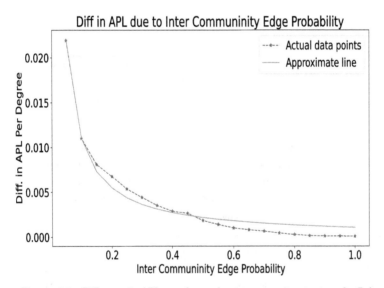

Figure 6.2: Difference in APL per degree due to community structure for Relaxed Caveman graph

difference in the value is 2.14% only, hence the proposed method is being used for the calculations of average shortest path lengths in the other sections.

6.3 Relation Between Community Structure and APL

To evaluate the relationship between community structure and average shortest path length, Relaxed Caveman and Planted Partition graphs comprising of 400 nodes with 20 communities each, are used for the experiment. The Relaxed Caveman graphs are

Chapter 6. Effect of Varying Community Structure on Network

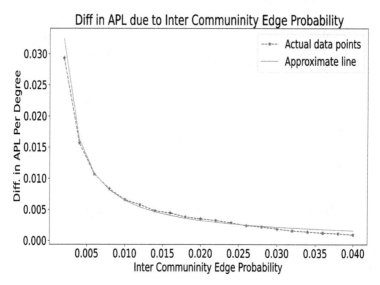

Figure 6.3: Difference in average path length per degree due to community structure for Planted Partition graph

constructed by varying the edge-rewiring probability (Probability of rewiring each edge to link to different communities) from 0.05 to 1.0. The Planted Partition graphs are constructed by varying the inter-community node-link probability from 0.002 to 0.04. The community structures in the Relaxed Caveman and Planted Partition graphs are distorted gradually by increasing the edge rewiring and inter-community node-link probabilities, respectively. The data presented in Table 6.2 & Table 6.3 contain number of nodes, edges, communities (20 communities are fixed for each graph), average node degree, APL of a Random graph (having equal number of nodes and edges), APL of the graph under study, difference in APLs, difference in APLs in fractions (calculated as [avg path length − random path length/random path length]), difference of path lengths in fractions per average degree. To normalize the effect of node degrees on average path lengths, the difference in average path lengths in fractions per average degree is calculated and presented in Figure 6.2 and Figure 6.3. The $x-axis$ is edge rewiring probability in figure 6.2 and inter-community node-link probability in Figure 6.3. The $y-axis$ is the difference in average shortest path lengths in fractions per degree. For both the figures, dashed blue lines represent actual data points, whereas solid red lines represent the approximated lines ($y = 0.002/x$ and $y = 0.00015/x$ in Figure 6.2 and 6.3).

Table 6.2: Relationship Between Community Structure and Average Shortest Path Length for Relaxed Caveman Graph

Nodes	Edges	Avg Deg	Communities	Inter Comm Prob	Rand Path Len	Avg Path Len	Difference	Diff in Frac	Diff in Frac Per Deg
400	3800	19	20	0.05	2.338191729	3.312719298	0.9745277569	0.416786851	0.02193615
400	3800	19	20	0.1	2.338191729	2.827105263	0.488913534	0.209098992	0.01100521
400	3800	19	20	0.15	2.338191729	2.698433584	0.360241855	0.154068569	0.008108872
400	3800	19	20	0.2	2.338191729	2.639122807	0.300931078	0.128702481	0.006773815
400	3800	19	20	0.25	2.338191729	2.577180451	0.238988722	0.102210917	0.005379522
400	3800	19	20	0.3	2.338191729	2.535538847	0.197347118	0.084401598	0.004442189
400	3800	19	20	0.35	2.338191729	2.495651629	0.1574599	0.067342595	0.003544347
400	3800	19	20	0.4	2.338191729	2.467117794	0.128926065	0.055139219	0.002902064
400	3800	19	20	0.45	2.338191729	2.456766917	0.118575188	0.050712346	0.002669071
400	3800	19	20	0.5	2.338191729	2.420526316	0.082334586	0.035212932	0.001853312
400	3800	19	20	0.55	2.338191729	2.401679198	0.063487469	0.027152379	0.001429073
400	3800	19	20	0.6	2.338191729	2.384260652	0.046068922	0.019702799	0.001036989
400	3800	19	20	0.65	2.338191729	2.37547619	0.037284461	0.015945853	0.000839255
400	3800	19	20	0.7	2.338191729	2.36839599	0.030204261	0.012917786	0.000679883
400	3800	19	20	0.75	2.338191729	2.359273183	0.021081454	0.009016136	0.000474533
400	3800	19	20	0.8	2.338191729	2.351578947	0.013387218	0.005725458	0.00030134
400	3800	19	20	0.85	2.338191729	2.34556391	0.00737218	0.003152941	0.000165944
400	3800	19	20	0.9	2.338191729	2.343834586	0.005642857	0.002413342	0.000127018
400	3800	19	20	0.95	2.338191729	2.343561404	0.005369674	0.002296507	0.000120869
400	3800	19	20	1	2.338191729	2.342208772	0.004017043	0.001718012	9.04217E-05

Chapter 6. *Effect of Varying Community Structure on Network* 95

Table 6.3: Relationship Between Community Structure and Average Shortest Path Length for Planted Partition Graph

Nodes	Edges	Avg Deg	Communities	Inter Comm Prob	Rand path len	Actual path len	Difference	Diff in Frac	Diff in Frac per Deg
400	2990	14.95	20	0.002	2.51516792	3.618634085	1.103466165	0.43872465	0.02934613
400	3107	15.535	20	0.004	2.487949875	3.092468672	0.604518797	0.242978688	0.015640727
400	3331	16.655	20	0.006	2.437860902	2.871553885	0.433692982	0.177898986	0.010681416
400	3439	17.195	20	0.008	2.413505013	2.758120301	0.344615288	0.142786233	0.008303939
400	3586	17.93	20	0.01	2.382794486	2.664298246	0.281503759	0.118140176	0.006588967
400	3753	18.765	20	0.012	2.348239348	2.603283208	0.25504386	0.108610675	0.005787939
400	3990	19.95	20	0.014	2.300929825	2.521766917	0.220837093	0.095977326	0.004810894
400	4056	20.28	20	0.016	2.288347118	2.495313283	0.206966165	0.090443519	0.00445974
400	4182	20.91	20	0.018	2.264525063	2.445814536	0.181289474	0.080056289	0.003828613
400	4366	21.83	20	0.02	2.232086466	2.403922306	0.17183584	0.076984401	0.003526542
400	4487	22.435	20	0.022	2.210743108	2.372318296	0.161575188	0.07308637	0.003257694
400	4625	23.125	20	0.024	2.188458722	2.334573935	0.146085213	0.066751641	0.002886557
400	4838	24.19	20	0.026	2.157645363	2.283972431	0.126327068	0.058548578	0.002420363
400	4988	24.94	20	0.028	2.134978697	2.252531328	0.117552632	0.05506033	0.002207712
400	5126	25.63	20	0.03	2.11608396	2.217581454	0.101497494	0.047964776	0.001871431
400	5368	26.84	20	0.032	2.085890977	2.174360902	0.088469925	0.042413494	0.001580235
400	5445	27.225	20	0.034	2.076695489	2.156629073	0.079933584	0.038490758	0.001413802
400	5580	27.9	20	0.036	2.062868421	2.133884712	0.071016291	0.034425992	0.001233907
400	5726	28.63	20	0.038	2.046467419	2.112418546	0.065951128	0.032226815	0.001125631
400	5937	29.685	20	0.04	2.026511278	2.083659148	0.05714787	0.028200124	0.000949979

Chapter 6. *Effect of Varying Community Structure on Network* 96

Table 6.4: Mean Community Size and Average Shortest Path Length Relationship for Relaxed Caveman Graph

Nodes	Edges	Avg Deg	No of Comm	Comm Size	Rand Path Len	Actual Path Len	Difference	Diff in Frac	Diff in Frac per Deg
180	450	5	30	6	3.414307883	6.763563004	3.349255121	0.980947013	0.196189403
245	735	6	35	7	3.262893108	5.666042155	2.403149047	0.736508665	0.122751444
256	896	7	32	8	3.056608456	4.910171569	1.853563113	0.606411694	0.086630242
270	1080	8	30	9	2.912182294	4.824810684	1.912628390	0.656768086	0.082096011
400	1800	9	40	10	2.960002785	4.315601504	1.355598719	0.457972109	0.05088579
396	1980	10	36	11	2.837014448	4.224472574	1.387458126	0.489055714	0.048905571
396	2178	11	33	12	2.745072241	4.030405319	1.285333078	0.462332879	0.042566625
403	2418	12	31	13	2.679376072	3.65433379	0.974957718	0.363874906	0.030322909
406	2639	13	29	14	2.620166636	3.432804233	0.812637597	0.310147296	0.023857484
405	2835	14	27	15	2.56626696	3.412907957	0.846640997	0.329911506	0.023565108
400	3000	15	25	16	2.512823308	3.251441604	0.738592732	0.293929434	0.019595296
391	3128	16	23	17	2.457864778	3.145517739	0.687652961	0.279776563	0.017486035
396	3366	17	22	18	2.418358266	3.087789285	0.669431019	0.276812178	0.016283069
399	3591	18	21	19	2.377818919	2.931965592	0.554146673	0.233048307	0.012947128
400	3800	19	20	20	2.3379198	2.834937343	0.497017544	0.212589647	0.011188929
399	3990	20	19	21	2.297727988	2.774927268	0.47719928	0.207683103	0.010384155
396	4158	21	18	22	2.257236223	2.766794528	0.509432298	0.225677592	0.010746472
408	4692	23	17	24	2.202213711	2.720503926	0.518290215	0.235349645	0.010232593
400	4800	24	16	25	2.162045113	2.676253133	0.51420802	0.237834085	0.009909754
390	5655	29	13	30	2.031768506	2.536365434	0.504596928	0.248353554	0.008563916
396	6930	35	11	36	1.952266974	2.413259174	0.4609922	0.236131742	0.006746621
400	7800	39	10	40	1.921743108	2.347982456	0.426239348	0.221798297	0.005687136
400	9800	49	8	50	1.879264411	2.165100251	0.28583584	0.152099852	0.003104079
400	15800	79	5	80	1.802005013	1.835463659	0.033458647	0.018567455	0.000235031
400	19800	99	4	100	1.751879699	1.762468672	0.010588972	0.006044349	6.1054E-05
400	39800	199	2	200	1.501253133	1.501365915	0.000112782	7.51252E-05	3.77514E-07

Chapter 6. *Effect of Varying Community Structure on Network* 97

Table 6.5: Mean Community Size and Average Shortest Path Length Relationship for Planted Partition Graph

Nodes	Edges	Avg Deg	No of Comm	Comm Size	Rand Path Len	Actual Path Len	Difference	Diff in Frac	Diff in Frac per Deg
180	409	4.544444444	30	6	3.599410304	5.402979516	1.803569212	0.501073526	0.110260678
245	675	5.510204082	35	7	3.41175421	4.719739043	1.307984833	0.383376044	0.069575652
256	797	6.2265625	32	8	3.242902369	4.449387255	1.206484886	0.372038609	0.059750241
270	958	7.096296296	30	9	3.067079719	3.921767865	0.854681845	0.278665122	0.039926093
400	1692	8.46	40	10	3.037382206	3.659824561	0.622442356	0.204927241	0.024223078
396	1867	9.429292929	36	11	2.90209564	3.526633423	0.624537783	0.215202344	0.022822745
396	2017	10.18686869	33	12	2.819677791	3.416762562	0.597084772	0.211756384	0.020787191
403	2227	11.05210918	31	13	2.748850043	3.312766194	0.563916151	0.205146204	0.018561724
392	2272	11.59183673	28	14	2.696356804	3.261065296	0.564708492	0.209433889	0.01806736
405	2532	12.5037037	27	15	2.649501283	3.175333089	0.525831805	0.198464446	0.015872453
400	2636	13.18	25	16	2.605685464	3.112506266	0.506820802	0.194505749	0.014757644
408	2855	13.99509804	24	17	2.569529556	3.065566797	0.49603724	0.193045937	0.013793825
396	2908	14.68686869	22	18	2.535622567	3.030609257	0.49498669	0.195213079	0.013291675
399	3165	15.86466165	21	19	2.471350487	2.885845266	0.41449478	0.16771995	0.010571921
400	3347	16.735	20	20	2.434918546	2.845338346	0.4104198	0.168555864	0.010072056
399	3484	17.46365915	19	21	2.401052883	2.791954761	0.390901878	0.16280436	0.009322466
396	3686	18.61616162	18	22	2.349405447	2.713438179	0.364032732	0.154946747	0.008323238
408	4217	20.67156863	17	24	2.281995231	2.635100352	0.353105121	0.154735258	0.007485414
400	4328	21.64	16	25	2.239347118	2.572556391	0.333209273	0.148797509	0.00687604
390	5263	26.98974359	13	30	2.074332608	2.382281985	0.307949377	0.148457087	0.0055005
396	6590	33.28282828	11	36	1.97098325	2.192392277	0.221409027	0.112334302	0.003375143
400	7688	38.44	10	40	1.925901003	2.068684211	0.142783208	0.074138394	0.001928678
400	9774	48.87	8	50	1.879709273	1.924536341	0.044827068	0.023847873	0.000487986
400	15087	75.435	5	80	1.810941103	1.811516291	0.000575188	0.000317618	4.21049E-06
400	18025	90.125	4	100	1.774122807	1.774223058	0.000100251	5.65071E-05	6.26986E-07
400	33803	169.015	2	200	1.576403509	1.576403512	3E-09	1.90307E-09	1.12597E-11

It can be seen from Table 6.2 & Table 6.3; for each graph, the APL is greater than the APL of a random graph having equal nodes and edges. As the community structure gets distorted, the difference of APL per degree is also reduced. From Figure 6.2 & Figure 6.3, it can be concluded that the difference in APL per degree is inversely proportional to the community structure in a network.

6.4 Mean Community Size and APL Relationship

In this section, the analysis is done to explore the relationship between the average path length of a network to the number of communities, mean sizes of communities, and average degree of nodes.

6.4.1 Number of Communities and APL

A line graph is plotted (as represented in Figure 6.4) with the number of communities as x-axis (community sizes varying from 2 to 40) and the difference in APL per average degree, in comparison with a random Erdos-Renyi graph with equal nodes and edges (shown in Table 6.4 and Table 6.5). Figure 6.4 shows the plots for both Relaxed Caveman and Planted Partition Graphs. For all these graphs, the number of nodes are approximately 400. From Figure 6.4 it can be inferred that, difference in average shortest path length per degree (with respect to a random graph) increases (nearly linear) with an increase in the number of communities of a graph.

6.4.2 Mean Size of Communities and APL

In this work, the impact of community sizes on average path length is investigated by varying the sizes from 6 to 200 with relaxed caveman and planted partition graphs (tabulated in Table 6.4 and Table 6.5). Relationship between the average community sizes with difference in average shortest path length per average degree is plotted in Figure 6.5. It can be seen in, the line plots of Relaxed Caveman and planted partition graphs match very closely to the approximate line $y = 5.0 \times x^{-2}$. The relationship between average shortest path lengths per degree and the community size is defined by Equation 6.4.1.

$$\text{difference in avg shortest path length per avg degree} = 5.0 \times \text{community\_size}^{-2}$$
(6.4.1)

Equation 6.4.1 can be modified to predict the average size of communities in a graph, as given by equation 6.4.2.

$$\text{community\_size} = \left[\frac{5.0}{\text{difference in avg shortest path length per avg degree}}\right]^{0.5}$$
(6.4.2)

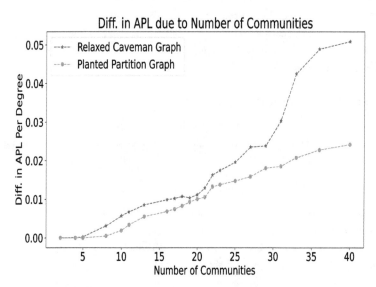

Figure 6.4: Difference in average shortest path length per degree due to number of communities present in the graph

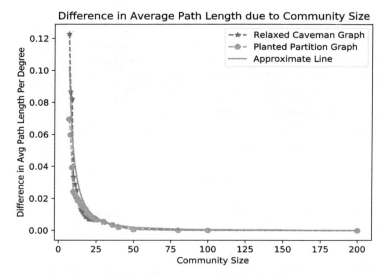

Figure 6.5: Difference in APL Per Degree due to Size of Communities in Graph

Once the average size of a community is calculated, total number of communities can also be found as given by equation 6.4.3:

$$Number\ of\ Communties = \frac{Number\ of\ Nodes}{community\_size} \quad (6.4.3)$$

Therefore, it can be concluded that, the number of communities and average size of communities of a graph can be predicted if the average shortest path length of a network is known.

6.4.3 Relationship between Average Degree of Community and APL

In this section, the average node degree of communities of graphs is compared with their average shortest path lengths. For this experiment, Relaxed Caveman graph and Planted Partition Graphs having 400 nodes and 20 communities are used. The Relaxed Caveman graphs are generated by varying probability of inter-community link, and Planted Partition Graphs are generated by varying probability of inter community nodes' link. Table 6.2 stores the data for Relaxed Caveman Graphs, and Table 6.3 stores data for Planted Partition Graphs. Both the tables contain total of nodes, total edges, and average degree of nodes inside the graph, APL, APL of a random Erdos-Renyi graph, the difference of path lengths in ratio, average node degrees inside the communities. $X - axis$ of the plot, in Figure 6.6 is represented as:

$\frac{Average\ Shotrest\ Path\ Length\ of\ Graph\ -\ Average\ Shotrest\ Path\ Length\ of\ Ranodm\ Graph}{Average\ Shortest\ Path\ Length\ of\ the\ Ranodm\ Graph}$

and $Y - axis$ represents:

$\frac{Average\ Degree\ of\ Nodes\ Inside\ Communities}{Average\ Degree\ of\ Nodes\ of\ the\ Graph}$

The blue dashed line is for Relaxed Caveman graph, the red dashed line is for Planted Partition graph, and the solid green line is an approximate line which matches very closely with the other two lines. The following equation gives the approximate line:

$$y = 1.0 - \frac{0.72}{2.0^{\frac{x}{0.072}}} \quad (6.4.4)$$

From this experiment, it can be concluded that, as the ratio of the difference in average shortest path length with respect to a random graph increases, the ratio between average node degrees of communities and average node degrees of the graph increases as well. The relationship presented in Equation 6.4.4 can be used to calculate the average degree of nodes inside communities without actually detecting the communities.

Example

Four graphs, each containing 12 nodes are shown in Figure 6.7, Figure 6.8, Figure 6.9 and Figure 6.10. The graph shown in Figure 6.7 has 14 edges and three communities of

Chapter 6. Effect of Varying Community Structure on Network

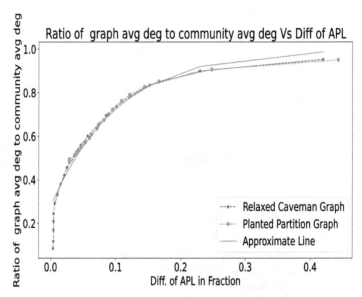

Figure 6.6: Relationship between difference in APL to ratio of average community degree and average graph degree

Table 6.6: Average Shortest Path Lengths

Graph	Number of Nodes	Number of Edges	Average Path Length
Graph-1	12	14	3.272727272727273
Graph-2	12	13	3.0
Graph-3	12	13	2.8484848484848486
Graph-4	12	13	2.696969696969697

equal sizes. The APL of this graph is 3.272727272727273. The graph presented in Figure 6.8 has 13 edges and two communities of similar sizes (six nodes each). The APL of this graph is 3.0. The community structure of Figure 6.8 is disrupted by replacing the edge connecting node 4 and node 5 with a new edge connecting node 4 and node 1, as shown in Figure 6.9. This graph has an APL 2.8484848484848486. The graph shown in Figure 6.10 has the same number of edges as of the previous graphs (13 edges), but the community structure is further disrupted; edge (9, 10) is replaced with the edge (7, 10). The APL of this graph is now reduced to 2.696969696969697.

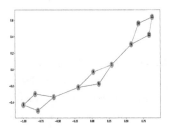

Figure 6.7: Graph with Three Communities

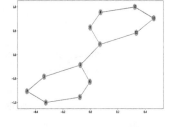

Figure 6.8: Graph with Two Communities

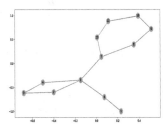

Figure 6.9: Graph with one edge reconnected

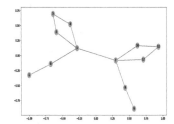

Figure 6.10: Graph with two edges reconnected

6.5 Connectivity Probability of two arbitrary Nodes belonging to a Community

Let the community inside graph G (N nodes and E edges) is C. Let the subgraph g, induced by the nodes of C, contains n nodes with e edges and a be the average node degree of the subgraph g. The value of a is defined by equation 6.5.1:

$$a = \frac{1}{\sum_{\forall i \in g} G.degree(i)} \qquad (6.5.1)$$

Let $Node1$ and $Node2$ are two nodes inside community C. If R is assumed to be two; the probability P that the nodes $Node1$ and $Node2$ are connected is the addition of the probability P_1 that the nodes are connected by an edge and the probability P_2 that the nodes are connected by an intermediate node ($2 - edge$ distance). The value of P is

Chapter 6. *Effect of Varying Community Structure on Network* 103

defined by the following equation:

$$P = P_1 + P_2 + P_3 + ... + P_R \qquad (6.5.2)$$

where P_R is the probability of a node connected with a source node with radius R. Though radius of a graph is generally defined as minimum eccentricity; however in this work, the radius R of subgraph g is defined as average distance between all the nodes. The connectivity probability is calculated by summing up to $R - edge$ distance, since R is the average distance in community g. The generalized probability P_R, for any arbitrary value of R is given in Equation 6.5.3.

$$P_R = \left(\frac{a^2}{a^2 + (n-a-1)*(n-a-2)} \right)^R * (n-2)*(n-3)*...*(n-R) \qquad (6.5.3)$$

6.5.1 Expressing the Probability in terms of number of Community Nodes

For this work, a term $sparsity(k)$ of a graph (inverse of graph density) is defined as, $k = n/a$. The value of k can be used to define a as, $a = n/k$, where the n members are there in the community. A special case where $k = 1$, the community becomes a clique. Substituting $a = n/k$ in equations 6.5.2 and 6.5.3, the value of P is defined as:

$$P \geq \frac{1}{k^2 - 2k + 2} + \frac{n-2}{(k^2 - 2k + 2)^2} + ... + \frac{(n-2)(n-3)...(n-R)}{(k^2 - 2k + 2)^R} \qquad (6.5.4)$$

Probability $P >= 1.0$ implies, there is a path between $Node1$ and $Node2$ inside community C. Since it is highly unlikely that, any arbitrary two nodes in a community do not have any path between them, so the probability value $P >= 1.0$ for any two community nodes. Based on the above discussions and analysis, an algorithm is designed to compute the radius of a community, which is described below. In the above algorithm, p_0 is the probability of connection between any two arbitrary nodes of the community. p is the probability of $i - length$ shortest path between two nodes of the community for the ith iteration.

6.6 The Proposed Technique for Community Detection

The proposed community detection algorithm is an enhancement over the proposed FSA algorithm in Chapter 4, by employing the finding presented in the previous sections of this chapter. The algorithm is named as Enhanced FSA (EFSA) whichs consists of two phases. EFSA picks an arbitrary seed node in the first phase, and it selects those nodes

Chapter 6. Effect of Varying Community Structure on Network

---

community_radius(n, a):

Data : total nodes n and Avg degree a of the community
Result: Radius of a community
$k = n/a$
$p_0 = \frac{1}{k^2 - 2k + 2}$
$p = p_0$
$P = p$
$R = 1$
while i *ranges from 2 to n-1* **do**
    if $P \geq 1.0$ **then**
        break
    else
        $p = (1 - P) * P * p_0 * (n - i)$
        $P = P + p$
        $R = i$
    end
end
return R

Algorithm 6: Computation of Radius of a Community

---

which are R-edge distance from it(R-radius neighborhood). The value of R is calculated using Algorithm 6 (community_radius(n,a)). The target is now to find all the other members of the community. The subgraph g, induced by the R-radius neighborhood nodes, contains both nodes belonging to the community and the nodes not belonging to the community. Now the search can be localized only to subgraph g rather the whole graph G. The next task is to filter out the non-community nodes from subgraph g, for which a Community Membership Matrix M is calculated. The Community Membership Matrix M is an adjacency matrix of g divided by degree of the node, and the diagonal entries of the matrix are set to 0.0. (The diagonal entries are set to zero since a node can't act as an intermediate node for a path involving the same node as an end-node.)

The algorithm finds communities repetitively by selecting different seed nodes randomly.The proposed algorithm does not restrict a node to have multiple community membership. However, a node belonging to any of the so far discovered communities is prohibited from being chosen as a seed node for detection of other communities, to ensures the algorithm stops after finite runs.

6.6.1 Phase-1: Choosing Arbitrary Seed and Finding R-radius Neighborhood

Let there is a graph G with N, E as total nodes and edges respectively, on which community detection has to be performed. To compute the appropriate value of radius R, the APL dis_G of G and the APL of a random graph dis_{rand} (a random graph having equal nodes and edges and using Algorithm 5) is needed to be calculated. Then the avg degree

Figure 6.11: Original Planted Partition Graph with 40 Nodes

of nodes d of the graph is calculated, the mean size of communities (S) and the number of communities (c) are also predicted using equation 6.4.2 and 6.4.3, respectively. Equation 6.4.4 is employed to predict the ratio of the average node degree of the community to the average node degree of the graph (y). Since the value of d of the graph is known, the average node degree of the community (a) can be calculated as $a = d \times y$. Algorithm 6 (community_radius(S, a)) is called to compute the approximate radius R of the community. Once the value of R is computed, the proposed algorithm extracts an R-radius neighborhood subgraph for randomly chosen seed node (s) from graph G. A Planted Partition Graph of 40 nodes and 4 communities is taken as an example (Figure 6.11). Each community contains 10 number of nodes. The average shortest path length dis_G of this graph is 2.34358974359, and the average shortest path length of the random graph, dis_{rand} is 1.93358974359 (Using Algorithm 5). Average node degree of G is found to be 8.25. Based on Equation 6.4.2 and 6.4.3, the mean size of communities S is $10.030441470721067 \approx 10$, and the number of communities c is $3.987860366541223 \approx 4$. Based on Equation 6.4.4, the average node degree of community a is 7.54256669741. Using Algorithm 6, the value of R is found to be 2.

Nodes in G are numbered from $0, 1, 2...., 39$. If the randomly chosen seed node is 10, then the 2-radius subgraph g of seed 10 contains the following nodes (total 21 nodes). $[10, 1, 6, 7, 11, 12, 13, 14, 15, 16, 17, 18, 19, 30, 32, 33, 34, 35, 36, 37, 38]$.
The second phase of the algorithm involves filtering out the non-community nodes $([1, 6, 7, 30, 32, 33, 34, 35, 36, 37, 38])$ from g.

Figure 6.12: Two-radius Subgraph of Seed Node '10'

6.6.2 Phase-2: Filtering out Non-Community Nodes from R-radius Subgraph

Once the R-radius subgraph g of graph G with a specific seed node is obtained, the Adjacency_matrix (A) of g is determined. A new matrix M (community membership matrix) having n rows and n columns (g has n nodes) is defined. Each entry $M[i][j]$ of M signifies the probability of jth node to be the part of community, if i^{th} node is a member of the community with 1-radius neighborhood (connected by an edge directly). The entries $M[i][j]$ of M is defined as follows:

$$M[i][j] = \begin{cases} \frac{A[i][j]}{G.degree(Node_j)} & \text{if } i \neq j \\ 0.0 & \text{if } i = j \end{cases} \qquad (6.6.1)$$

For a community C, contained inside R-radius neighborhood of seed; $M[i][j]$ is a conditional probability value of jth Node to be a part of community if i^{th} Node is a part of community C, which can be expressed as:

$$M[i][j] = probability\left[j^{th}\ Node\ \in C | i^{th}\ Node\ \in C\right] \qquad (6.6.2)$$

Similarly, the value of $M^2[i][j]$ may be expressed in terms of conditional probability.

$$M^2[i][j] = \sum_{\forall k \in N(j)} prob\left[j^{th}\ Node\ \in C | k^{th}\ Node\ \in C\right] \times prob\left[k^{th}\ Node\ \in C | i^{th}\ Node\ \in C\right]$$

$$(6.6.3)$$

where, N(j) is the set of neighbor nodes of jth Node.
For the next operations, M^R is calculated from M. Each entry $M^R[i][j]$ of matrix M^R signifies the probability of jth node to be part of community, if the ith node is a member

of the community. This implies the shortest path between j^{th} node and i^{th} node is R and there are $(R-2)$ number of intermediate nodes along the path. The value of $M^R[i][j]$ can be computed using the Markov model.

$$M^R[i][j] = \text{probability}\left[j^{th}\,Node \in C | (R-2)^{th} Node \in C, (R-3)^{th} Node \in C..., i^{th}\,Node \in C\right]$$
$$= \sum_{\forall node \in N(j)} \text{probability}\left[j^{th}\,Node \in C | (R-2)^{th} Node \in C\right]$$

(6.6.4)

In the above equation, $(R-2)^{th} Node, (R-3)^{th} Node$...... are $R-2$ numbers of intermediate nodes and N(j) is set of neighbor nodes of jth Node.

Since the seed node s is the first node of subgraph g, the first row of M^R is only considered for community detection. The entry of matrix M^R at [0][0] is explicitly set to 1.0 as $M^R[0][0]$ is the membership value of the seed node. Let's denote the first row of the community as row_1. Sort row_1 according to their membership values in descending order. Obviously the seed node will have maximum membership value(1.0) and the community members will have high membership values compared to the non-members. In order to filter out the non-members, searching for the steep decrease in membership values is needed. A list L of size n is defined, whose entries are defined as:

$$L[i] = \begin{cases} 1.0 & \text{if } i = 1 \\ \frac{row_1[i]}{row_1[i-1]} & \text{if } i \geq 2 \end{cases}$$

(6.6.5)

The maximum value of $L[i]$ will be 1.0 for the first entry, and all the other values will be less than or equal to 1.0. Searching is done for the index of L, which stores the minimum value of $L[i]$. This index i is the inflection point; nodes stored at indexes less than index i are community members, and the others are non-members.

The algorithm runs till all the nodes of G are assigned to at least one community. The second phase of the algorithm is executed repetitively with different seed nodes. The seed nodes are chosen from the nodes not part of any community discovered so-far. Once all the nodes are assigned to at least one community, there will be no seed left to continue, and the community detection process will stop. Though the selection of seed is restricted only to non-member nodes, the community nodes discovered by the seed nodes are not restricted. A node assigned to one community may be assigned to other communities, if it is rediscovered by some other seed nodes. Therefore, the algorithm works with overlapping community structure by assigning some of the nodes to more than one communities.

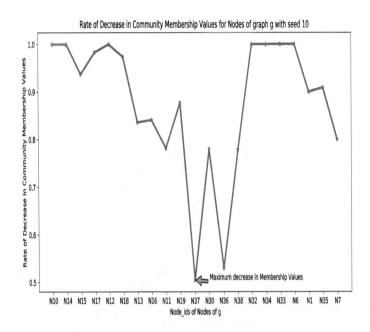

Figure 6.13: Decrease in Membership Values for Nodes of Subgraph g and Seed 10

Figure 6.14: Community 1

Figure 6.15: Community 2

Chapter 6. Effect of Varying Community Structure on Network

Figure 6.16: Community 3   **Figure 6.17:** Community 4

The same example is continued in this subsection (Planted Partition Graph with 40 nodes 4 communities and with seed node 10). The value of M^2 (as $R = 2$) is calculated and the first row of the matrix (signifies the community memberships of nodes with seed '10'), sorted in decreasing order of membership values along with their respective node_ids are given as belows:

$((10, 1.0), (14, 0.19826388888888888), (15, 0.1857638888888889), (17, 0.18263888888888888),$
$(12, 0.18263888888888888), (18, 0.17777777777777776), (13, 0.14861111111111114), (16,$
$0.125), (11, 0.09768518518518518), \quad (19, 0.08571428571428572), (37, 0.04326388888888888),$
$(30, 0.03373015873015873), (36, 0.017857142857143), (38, 0.01388888888888), (32, 0.013888888888$
$(34, \ 0.01388888888888), (33, \ 0.01388888888888), (6, \ 0.01388888888888), (1, \ 0.0125), (35,$
$0.011363636363636364), (7, 0.009090909090909092))$

The value of L is calculated as defined in Equation 6.6.5 and represented as a plot between *node_ids* and the entries of L are shown in Figure 6.9. It can be seen in Figure 6.9, there is a steep decrease in the membership value of L at Node 37, and a bisection point of the list is obtained. Nodes $[10, 11, 12, 13, 14, 15, 16, 17, 18, 19]$ are included in the community while $[1, 6, 7, 30, 32, 33, 34, 35, 36, 37, 38]$ are excluded. The algorithm is executed fully, and the four communities are detected. The communities are shown in Figure 6.14, Figure 6.15, Figure 6.16 and Figure 6.17 respectively.

6.6.3 The Algorithm for Community Detection

The community discovery algorithm is divided in to two parts. The part-2 is referred as Local Community Detection Algorithm, as it identified communities locally for a given seed node. This algorithm is called by the Community_detection algorithm to detect all the communities of a network.

```
local_community_detection(G, g, R):
Data : Graph G, Subgraph g, Radius R
Result: List of community nodes
n = no_of_nodes(g)
A = Adjacency_matrix(g)
M[n][n] = [ ][ ]                    ▶ Declare a n×n matrix
while i ranges from 1 to n do
    while j ranges from 1 to n do
        if i = j then
            M[i][j] = 1.0
        else
            M[i][j] = A[i][j] / G.degree(Node_j)
        end
    end
end
N = M^R                             ▶ membership value of R-radius subgraph
row_1 = N[1]                        ▶ first row of N
sorted(row_1)
L[n] = [ ]                          ▶ blank list of n elements
L[1] = [1.0]
while i in range 2 to n do
    L[i] = row_1[i]/row_1[i-1]
end
Min = 1.0                           ▶ stores minimum value of L[i]
I = 1                               ▶ stores index i of minimum value of L[i]
while i in range 1 to n do
    if L[i] < Min then
        Min = L[i]
        I = i
    else
    end
end
List = [nodes from 1 to I - 1]
return List
```
Algorithm 7: Local Community Detection Algorithm

6.6.4 Performance Evaluation of the Proposed Algorithm

In this subsection, the proposed algorithm is evaluated against five different widely used (Label_Propagation [**Raghavan et al.** (2007)],Greedy_modularity [**Newman** (2004)], Walktrap [**Pons and Latapy** (2006)], Multilevel [**Blondel et al.** (2008)] and Infomap [**Rosvall and Bergstrom** (2008)])community detection methods using conductance and modularity values. For this experimental work, we have employed real-world networks as well as synthetic networks. Specifications of these networks are described in Table 6.7 and Table 6.8, respectively. Ten iterations of each experiment are conducted, and the minimum, maximum, average values along with the standard deviations are tabulated in

Chapter 6. Effect of Varying Community Structure on Network

---

community_detection(G):

Data : Graph G
Result: List of communities
$N = no\_of\_nodes(G)$
$E = no\_of\_edges(G)$
$d = 2E/N$ ▶ average node degree of graph of G
$dis = avg\_shortest\_distance(G)$
$rnd = avg\_sht\_path\_len\_rndg(N, E)$ ▶ using Algorithm 1
$x = \frac{dis-rnd}{rnd}$
$y = 1.0 - \frac{0.72}{2.0^{\frac{x}{0.072}}}$
$a = y \times d$ ▶ average node degree of community
$z = x/d$
$Size = \left[\frac{5.0}{z}\right]^{0.5}$ ▶ mean community size of using Equation 7
$R = community\_radius(Size, a)$ ▶ radius using Algorithm 2
$List1 = nodes\_of(G)$
$List2 = [\ ]$ ▶ a blank list to store communities
$List3 = [\ ]$ ▶ a blank list to store a single community
while node s in $List1$ **do**
  if $s \notin List2$ **then**
    $g = R\_radius\_subgraph(G, R)$
    $List3 = local\_community\_detection(G, g, R)$ ▶ using Algo 3
    $List2.add(List3)$
  else
  end
end
return $List2$

Algorithm 8: Community Detection Algorithm

Tables 6.9-6.10 and Tables 6.11-6.12. The proposed algorithm is also compared with the FS algorithm [**Pattanayak et al.** (2019)] since the proposed algorithm is an enhancement over FSA. The results of the comparative analysis are tabulated in Table 6.13. The best values of modularity and conductance are highlighted using bold fonts.

For the synthetic networks, shown in Tables 6.9-6.10, the proposed algorithm performs best with conductance and modularity values for Barabasi Albert graph, Relaxed Caveman graph, Gaussian Random graph, LFR graph, and Planted Partition graph. For Newman Watts graph, the proposed algorithm has the best conductance score, whereas the Infomap algorithm has the best modularity score.

The proposed algorithm has better conductance and modularity scores across all the real-world networks, in comparison to other methods, shown in Tables 6.11-6.12.

There are convergences in conductance and modularity scores for the proposed algorithm and the FS algorithms, presented in Table 6.13. However, in few cases, the proposed algorithm performs better than FSA. For Gaussian Random graph, Newman

Table 6.7: Specifications for Synthetic Networks [**Pattanayak et al.** (2019)]

Network	Specifications
Barabasi Albert preferential attachment graph **Barabási and Albert** (1999)	1000 nodes with 11856 edges
Relaxed Caveman Graph **Watts** (2000)	1000 nodes with 50 communities, each having size 20, prob. of linking with distinct communities = 0.3
Gaussian Random Partition Graph	1500 nodes with 30 being avg. community size, prob. of intra-community link= 0.5 and prob. of inter-community link = 0.05
LFR Benchmark Graph**Lancichinetti and Fortunato** (2009)	2500 nodes, power law exponent of node degree=3.0, power law exponent of the community size=1.5, mean degree of nodes=10, minimum size of community =25, inter-community edges incident on each node = 0.25
Newman Watts Strogatz Graph**Newman et al.** (2001)	1000 nodes with each node having 20 neighbors
Planted Partition Graph**Mossel et al.** (2015)	1000 nodes divided into 50 communities, prob. of linking inside community= 0.5, prob. of linking with outside community=0.05

Table 6.8: Specifications for Real-World Networks [**Pattanayak et al.** (2019)]

Network	Specifications
Collaboration **Watts** (2000)	Co-authorship network of articles published in the area of relativity and quantum cosmology stored in arXiv database with 5242 nodes(scientists) and 14,446 edges(collaborations).
Netsc **Newman** (2006a)	Scientists collaborated in network science. 1589 nodes(scientists) and 2741 edges(co-authorship).
PGP **Boguná et al.** (2004)	Network of web-trust signature with private communication. 10680 nodes (web users) and 24316 edges (bi-directional signatures).
Twitter **Leskovec and Mcauley** (2012)	It is an online Social Network containing 23370 nodes(users) and 32831 edges(followings).
Yeast **Kim et al.** (2013)	A probabilistic functional gene network for Baker's yeast with 4172 nodes(genes) and 81953 edges (relations).
Facebook **Leskovec and Mcauley** (2012)	It is an online social network containing 2888 nodes(users) and 2981 edges(friendship).

Watts graph and in Yeast network, FSA performs better with modularity score whereas the proposed algorithm outperforms FSA in conductance score across all the networks.

Chapter 6. *Effect of Varying Community Structure on Network* 113

Table 6.9: Modularity and Conductance Scores of Synthetic Networks

Graph	Algorithm	Modularity				Conductance			
		Avg	Max	Min	SD	Avg	Max	Min	SD
Barbasi-Albert	Proposed	**0.462886809**	**0.462886809**	0.462886809	0.0	**0.372946961**	0.37299620	**0.37290529**	0.0
	Multilevel	0.43783840	0.43783840	0.43783840	0.0	0.39638362	0.39638362	0.39638362	0.0
	Label Prop	0.124591576	0.36604539	0.0	0.097767712	0.67299444	1.0	**0.24550898**	0.23360948
	Infomap	0.43570517	0.44210745	0.42887078	0.0037652544	0.4531048	0.46385399	0.44077122	0.00658832
	Greedy Mod.	0.41679248	0.41679248	0.41679248	0.0	0.4321058	0.43210580	0.4321058	0.0
	Walktrap	0.36870054	0.36870054	0.36870054	0.0	0.45056751	0.45056751	0.45056751	0.0
Relaxed Caveman	Proposed	**0.64645232**	**0.64645232**	0.64645232	0.0	**0.25407261**	0.25407261	**0.25407261**	0.0
	Multilevel	**0.64645432**	**0.64645432**	0.64645432	0.0	**0.25407261**	0.2540726	0.2540726	0.0
	Label Prop	0.6453669	0.36604539	0.63558024	0.0034386841	0.255466663	0.2560726	0.25801293	0.00191623
	Infomap	**0.64645432**	**0.64645432**	0.64645432	0.0	**0.25407261**	0.2540726	**0.2540726**	0.0
	Greedy Mod	0.60025925	0.60025925	0.60025925	0.0	0.2705183	0.2705183	0.2705183	0.0
	Walktrap	0.64156049	0.64156049	0.64156049	0.0	0.2570058	0.2570058	0.2570058	0.0
Gaussian Random	proposed	**0.35497142**	**0.35497142**	0.35497142	0.0	**0.12850812**	0.12850812	**0.12850812**	0.0
	Multilevel	0.35497142	0.35497142	0.35497142	0.0	**0.12850812**	0.12850812	**0.12850812**	0.0
	Label Prop	0.31947427	0.35497141	0.0	0.11225181	0.21565731	1.0	**0.12850812**	0.27558992
	Infomap	0.35497141	0.35497141	0.35497141	0.0	**0.12850812**	0.12850812	**0.12850812**	0.0
	Greedy Mod	0.35497141	0.35497141	0.35497141	0.0	**0.12850812**	0.12850812	**0.12850812**	0.0
	Walktrap	0.35497141	0.35497141	0.35497141	0.0	**0.12850812**	0.12850812	**0.12850812**	0.0

Table 6.10: Modularity and Conductance Scores of Synthetic Networks (In continuation of Table 6.9)

Graph	Algorithm	Modularity				Conductance			
		Avg	Max	Min	SD	Avg	Max	Min	SD
LFR	Proposed	**0.42831724**	**0.428380537**	0.42810277	2.92149E-05	**0.38216213**	0.38386548	**0.38194705**	3.9496E-05
	Multilevel	0.41581204	0.41581204	0.415812049557	0.0	0.39970851	0.399708518	0.39970851	0.0
	Label Prob	0.1145606537	0.323916494	0.0135211158	0.0932873074	0.024444444	0.24444444	**0.0**	0.073300120
	Infomap	0.39038007	0.39671341	0.38696813	0.0031059893	0.48545871	0.49015172	0.47628866	0.0042811215
	Greedy Mod	0.41730976	0.41730976	0.41730976	0.0	0.40157066	0.40157066	0.40157066	0.0
	Walktrap	0.34132427	0.34132427	0.34132427	0.0	0.46834257	0.46834257	0.468342579	0.0
Newman	Proposed	0.54310721	0.54318338	0.542892529	2.6602E-05	**0.14574852**	0.14578526	**0.14570514**	2.28005E-05
	Multilevel	0.50962641	0.50962641	0.50962641	0.0	0.1570302	0.1570302	0.1570302	0.0
	Label Prop	0.55955098	0.57352826	0.5412653	0.0110314	0.30658392	0.36122414	0.25771604	0.030233499
	Infomap	**0.59404136**	**0.59427986**	0.59308735	0.00050280581	0.23950963	0.24095096	0.2391493	0.00075964378
	Greedy Mod	0.51179638	0.51179638	0.51179638	0.0	0.14811205	0.14811205	0.14811205	0.0
	Walktrap	0.59005721	0.59005721	0.59005721	0.0	0.24449893	0.24449893	0.24449893	0.0
Planted	Proposed	**0.41214592**	**0.41214592**	0.41214592	0.0	**0.45721654**	0.45721654	**0.45721654**	0.0
	Multilevel	0.38425449	0.38425449	0.38425449	0.0	0.47130349	0.47130349	0.47130349	0.0
	Label Prop	0.10559975	0.39540598	0.0	0.17270796	0.83168483	1.0	**0.3559787**	0.27312732
	Infomap	0.39479953	0.39479953	0.39479953	0.0	0.5048392	0.5048392	0.5048392	0.0
	Greedy Mod	0.3636132	0.3636132	0.3636132	0.0	0.46820733	0.46820733	0.46820733	0.0
	Walktrap	0.37840099	0.37840099	0.37840099	0.0	0.54384223	0.54384223	0.54384223	0.0

Table 6.11: Modularity and Conductance Values for Real-World Networks

Graph	Algorithm	Modularity				Conductance			
		Avg	Max	Min	SD	Avg	Max	Min	SD
Collaboration	Proposed	**0.87294099**	**0.87294099**	0.87294099	0.0	**0.01042028**	0.01042028	**0.01042028**	0.0
	Multilevel	0.84125015	0.84125015	0.84125015	0.0	0.120707149	0.120707149	0.120707149	0.0
	Label Prop	0.79448988	0.8018414	0.79067722	0.003756012	0.13178136	0.13706353	0.127133332	0.00274261
	Infomap	0.79435193	0.79672198	0.79194442	0.00147729	0.12614283	0.12873627	0.12210227	0.00230815
	Greedy Mod	0.8045631	0.8045631	0.8045631	0.0	0.018230676	0.01823067	0.01823067	0.0
	Walktrap	0.78248973	0.78248973	0.78248973	0.0	0.15837981	0.15837981	0.15837981	0.0
Netsc	Proposed	**0.95862718**	**0.95868334**	0.95847742	1.73083E-05	**0.294443529**	0.29445133	**0.29442648**	6.9963E-06
	Multilevel	0.9577347	0.9577347	0.9577347	0.0	0.31621021	0.31621021	0.31621021	0.0
	Label Prop	0.90925477	0.92015184	0.89764481	0.00673972	0.30945147	0.31130499	0.30793506	0.00122439
	Infomap	0.92933269	0.93031907	0.92896023	0.00059732	0.30508458	0.30515111	0.30493696	8.35648 74e-05
	Greedy Mod	0.92933269	0.93031907	0.92896023	0.00059732	0.30508458	0.30515111	0.30493696	8.35648 74e-05
	Walktrap	0.95597277	0.95597277	0.955972 77	0.0	0.31148403	0.31148403	0.31148403	0.0
PGP	Proposed	**0.87174188**	**0.87174188**	0.87174188	0.0	**0.06537381**	0.06537381	**0.06537381**	0.0
	Multilevel	0.85958754	0.85958754	0.85958754	0.0	0.09262664	0.09262664	0.09262664	0.0
	Label Prop	0.8055388	0.8192046	0.7924703	0.0076508	0.18245328	0.18632097	0.17742624	0.00257085
	Infomap	0.80123501	0.80216304	0.79927435	0.00100482	0.1914648	0.19221963	0.19083542	0.00062013
	Greedy Mod	0.856452907	0.856452907	0.856452907	0.0	0.07271419	0.07271419	0.07271419	0.0
	Walktrap	0.7894202	0.7894202	0.7894202	0.0	0.24025269	0.24025269	0.24025269	0.0

Table 6.12: Modularity and Conductance Values for Real-World Networks (In continuation of Table 6.11)

Graph	Algorithm	Modularity				Conductance			
		Avg	Max	Min	SD	Avg	Max	Min	SD
Twitter	Proposed	**0.89661855**	**0.89661855**	0.89661855	0.0	**0.03835619**	0.03835619	**0.03835619**	0.0
	Multilevel	0.86623651	0.86623651	0.86623651	0.0	0.03974205	0.03974205	0.03974205	0.0
	Label Prop	0.79323543	0.80215134	0.78320292	0.00528305	0.19536893	0.20476605	0.18738220	0.00602302
	Infomap	0.82524101	0.82687861	0.82431713	0.00085536	0.18135357	0.18254362	0.17900480	0.00100699
	Greedy Mod	0.86934555	0.86934555	0.86934555	0.0	0.04250495	0.04250495	0.04250495	0.0
	Walktrap	0.85228512	0.85228512	0.85228512	0.0	0.10677522,	0.10677522	0.10677522	0.0
Yeast	Proposed	**0.68128793**	**0.68128793**	0.68128793	0.0	**0.08452807**	0.08452807	**0.08452807**	0.0
	Multilevel	0.66022337	0.66022337	0.66022337	0.0	0.130817534,	0.130817534	0.130817534	0.0
	Label Prop	0.61879314	0.63140643	0.59371545	0.01296553	0.27261272	0.29847784	0.24452698	0.02179358
	Infomap	0.62036554	0.62117961	0.6193235	0.00057629	0.36609700	0.37050573	0.36070922	0.00317259
	Greedy Mod	0.57000291	0.57000291	0.57000291	0.0	0.14736525	0.14736525	0.14736525	0.0
	Walktrap	0.63951646	0.63951646	0.63951646	0.0	0.44274368,	0.44274368	0.44274368	0.0
Facebook	Proposed	**0.80920512**	**0.80920512**	0.80920512	0.0	**0.08117634**	0.08117634	**0.08117634**	0.0
	Multilevel	0.8086875	0.8086875	0.8086875	0.0	0.12179438	0.12179438	0.12179438	0.0
	Label Prop	0.79516083	0.79991928	0.79426049	0.0016838239	0.163434325	0.167284267	0.141051065	0.0078959995
	Infomap	0.79612357	0.79612357	0.79612357	0.0	0.21754008	0.21754008	0.21754008	0.0
	Greedy Mod	0.80872175	0.80872175	0.80872175	0.0	0.12179826	0.12179826	0.12179826	0.0
	Walktrap	0.63305553	0.63305553	0.63305553	0.0	0.17201910	0.17201910	0.17201910	0.0

Table 6.13: Comparison of EFSA with FSA

Graph	Algorithm	Modularity				Conductance			
		Avg	Max	Min	SD	Avg	Max	Min	SD
Barbasi-Albert	Proposed	0.462886809	0.462886809	0.462886809	0.0	0.372946961	0.372996209	0.37290529	0.0
	FSA	0.462217475	0.46226524	0.46218886	2.49111E-05	0.375529236	0.375589143	0.37548263	3.46052E-05
Relaxed Caveman	Proposed	0.64645232	0.64645232	0.64645232	0.0	0.25407261	0.25407261	0.25407261	0.0
	FSA	0.64645232	0.64645232	0.64645232	0.0	0.25407261	0.25407261	0.25407261	0.0
Gaussian Random	Proposed	0.35497142	0.35497142	0.35497142	0.0	0.12850812	0.12850812	0.12850812	0.0
	FSA	0.36270018	0.36270018	0.36270018	0.0	0.13736295	0.13736295	0.13736295	0.0
LFR	Proposed	0.42831724	0.428380537	0.42810277	2.92149E-05	0.38216213	0.38386548	0.38194705	3.9496E-05
	FSA	0.421924071	0.42198445	0.42180986	4.54103E-05	0.391426709	0.39148834	0.39133682	4.5042E-05
Newman-Watts	Proposed	0.54310721	0.54318338	0.54292529	2.6602E-05	0.14574852	0.14578526	0.14570514	2.28005E-05
	FSA	0.612236177	0.611238903	0.61232487	2.08904E-05	0.226945372	0.226998582	0.22689334	3.38938E-05
Planted Partition	Proposed	0.41214592	0.41214592	0.41214592	0.0	0.45721654	0.45721654	0.45721654	0.0
	FSA	0.41214592	0.41214592	0.41214592	0.0	0.45721654	0.45721654	0.45721654	0.0
Collaboration	Proposed	0.87294099	0.87294099	0.87294099	0.0	0.01042028	0.01042028	0.01042028	0.0
	FSA	0.86153846	0.86153846	0.86153846	0.0	0.01068552	0.01068552	0.01068552	0.0
Netsc	Proposed	0.95862718	0.95868334	0.95847742	1.73083E-05	0.294435529	0.29445133	0.29442648	6.9963E-06
	FSA	0.958509905	0.95854258	0.95848811	1.76644E-05	0.300718662	0.30074131	0.30070856	8.7623E-06
PGP	Proposed	0.87174188	0.87174188	0.87174188	0.0	0.06537381	0.06537381	0.06537381	0.0
	FSA	0.87170003	0.87170003	0.87170003	0.0	0.06537782	0.06537782	0.06537782	0.0
Twitter	Proposed	0.89661855	0.89661855	0.89661855	0.0	0.03835619	0.03835619	0.03835619	0.0
	FSA	0.89661855	0.89661855	0.89661855	0.0	0.03835619	0.03835619	0.03835619	0.0
Yeast	Proposed	0.68128793	0.68128793	0.68128793	0.0	0.08452807	0.08452807	0.08452807	0.0
	FSA	0.681658361	0.681666955	0.68164109	7.8005E-06	0.084592892	0.08459804	0.08458625	4.34955E-06
Facebook	Proposed	0.80920512	0.80920512	0.809205123	0.0	0.08117634	0.08117634	0.08117634	0.0
	FSA	0.80745637	0.80745637	0.80745637	0.0	0.08133839	0.08133839	0.08133839	0.0

6.6.5 Comparison with LFR Benchmark Networks

LFR benchmark synthetic network is a randomly generated network with a predefined community structure. The mixing parameter (μ) in LFR is used to control the overlapping between communities. The μ values vary from 0.1 to 1.0 for the experiments. When the value of μ is greater than 0.5, the generated network's community structure becomes highly distorted.

In this experiment, FSA, Multilevel, Label Propagation, Infomap, Fastgreedy, Walktrap, and the proposed EFSA community detection algorithms are evaluated using LFR benchmark networks with varying mixing parameter values. There are two sets of networks. The first set of networks have 1000 nodes with exponent of power-law of degree distribution is 2.5, exponent of power-law controlling the variations of community size distribution is 1.5, average node degree and maximum node dgreee are 20 and 50 respectively. The size of communities are ranging from 25 to 50. Ten different networks of similar configurations are generated by varying the value of μ from 0.1 to 1.0.

The second set of networks have 5000 nodes with exponent of power-law of degree distribution is 2.5, exponent of power-law of degree distribution is 1.5. The average node degree and maximum node degrees are 20 and 50 respectively. Minimum and maximum size of the community is 25 and 100, respectively. the maximum size of the community is 100. The value of μ is varied between 0.1 to 1.0 to create 10 such networks.

The comparison of modularity and conductance values for all the evaluated algorithms on the two sets of networks (1000 and 5000 nodes) are shown in Figures 6.18 and 6.19, respectively.

Across all the synthetic networks, the modularity value decreases, and the conductance value increases with the increase in the mixing parameter μ. As shown in figure 6.18, EFSA,FSA, Multilevel, Fastgreedy, and Walktrap have similar performance for modularity and conductance. However, the performance of Label propagation and Infomap degrades rapidly for mixing parameter values greater than 0.5. Also, it can be noticed from Figure 6.19, EFSA,FSA, Multilevel, Fastgreedy algorithms perform similarly, while Label propagation, Infomap algorithms perform poorly both in-terms of modularity and conductance for mixing parameter values greater than 0.6.

In all the LFR benchmark networks, the proposed EFSA performs reasonably and competitively.

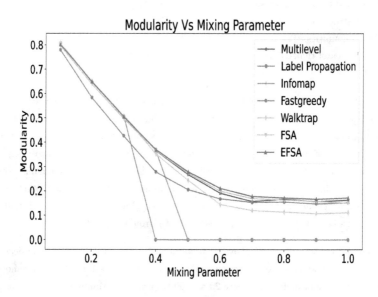

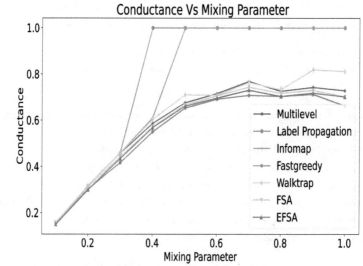

Figure 6.18: Modularity and Conductance for LFR network with 1000 nodes and Mixing parameter μ varies from 0.1 to 1.0.

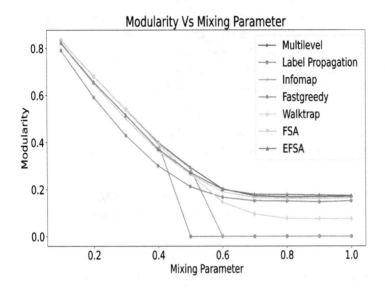

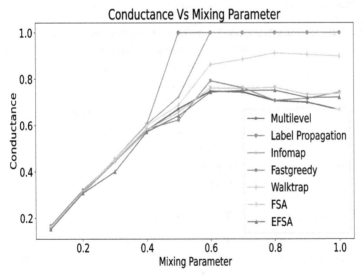

Figure 6.19: Modularity and Conductance LFR network with 5000 nodes and Mixing parameter μ varies from 0.1 to 1.0.

6.6.6 Comparison for Local Community Detection Algorithms

In this section, EFSA is compared with other local community detection algorithms, namely,FSA, LICOD [**Yakoubi and Kanawati (2014)**], HCLD [**Tabarzad and Hamzeh (2017)**], Local-T [**Fagnan et al. (2014)**], CDERS [**Lim and Datta (2013)**], and ENBC [**Biswas and Biswas (2015)**]. The experiments are conducted with ground-truth networks having predefined community membership. F_measure accuracy is used for the evaluation.The datasets used for the experiments with predefined community memberships are:

Zachary Karate Club [Zachary (1977)]: Social network dataset created by Zachary studying the 34 members of a Karate club. The social network has two communities.

Bottlenose Dolphin Network [Lusseau et al. (2003)]: Social network generated by studying the interaction of 62 Bottlenose Dolphins for seven years. It has two different communities.

American Political network [Krebs (2017)]: This social network is a network of 105 political books bought on Amazon by Americans. This network has three communities.

LFR Benchmark Network [Lancichinetti and Fortunato (2009)]: This synthetic network has 1000 nodes, 150740 edges, 152 communities. The minimum and average node degrees are 30 and 100, respectively. The minimum and maximum community sizes are 40 and 100, respectively. Mixing parameter is set to 0.1.

The F-measure of different local community detection algorithms compared and presented in Figures 6.20-6.23. In Karate Club, Bottlenose Dolphin, Political Book networks, EFSA has the best F-measure, and in the LFR benchmark graph, the proposed EFSA has the best F-measure along with FSA and HCLD. Across all the networks, the maximum F-measure value 1.0 is obtained only for synthetic network.

6.7 Adapting FSA to Work with Time Variant Networks

Time variant networks or dynamic networks introduce set of additional issues for community detection. In dynamic networks, the structure of the networks varies overtime. Some new nodes may be added to the exiting network, some nodes may no longer be the part of the network, some new links may be established between already exiting nodes and some previous links may get disconnected, overtime. The structure of the network and its connection between nodes at any point of time is called as snapshot of the network.

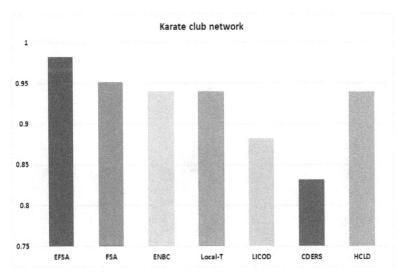

Figure 6.20: F_Score values for Karate club network

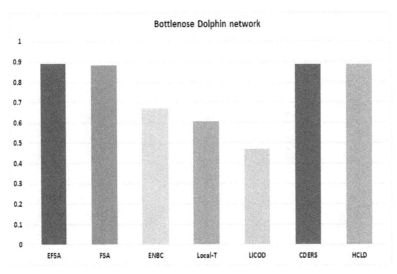

Figure 6.21: F_Score values for Bottelenose dolphin network

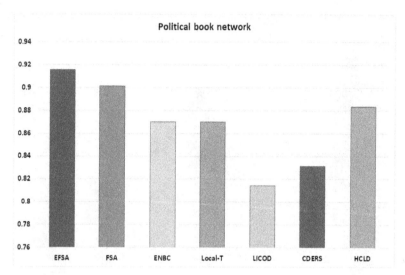

Figure 6.22: F_Score values for American political book Dolphin network

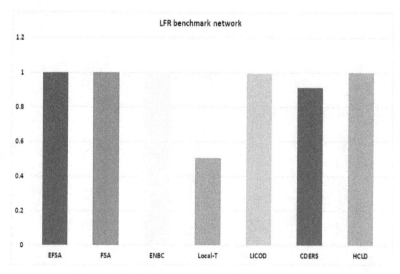

Figure 6.23: F_Score values for LFR Benchmark network

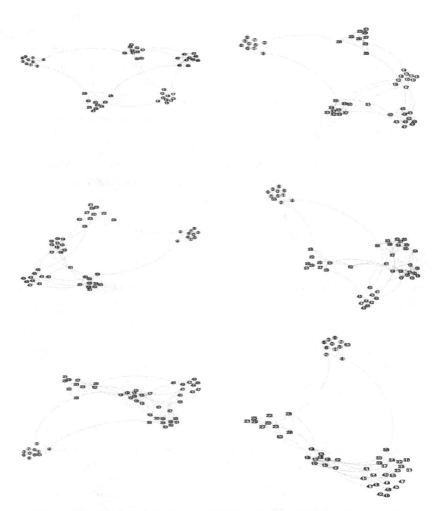

Figure 6.24: A time-variant network, initially had 5 communities, the edges and nodes changed over time and the last network has 4 communities.

Due to this change in structure of networks, the communities detected using community detection algorithms may no longer be valid after a interval of time and the network level community discovery may have to be redone. Another issue with the already existing algorithm is the determination of interval after which the community detection may be redone. We have designed a community detection method for dynamic networks derived from the already designed Fire Spread community detection algorithm. With this method, the Fire Spread community detection algorithm is executed initially at the network level to detect overall community structure of the network. An interval is decided to rerun the algorithm at the network level, depending on the level of dynamism in the network, which is of longer length. In between the longer length interval, there defined a shorter length interval, in which the networks checked for new connections, disconnections, new nodes added or deleted from the network.

For already exiting nodes along with their community memberships, we have defined threshold value , i.e, link_threshold which is set to 2% of the total links of the community for our experiment. If the changes of the links is above the link_threshold, then the local Fire Spread algorithm is rerun for the particular community with a seed node to check if the community structure is changed(i.e, the community is divided, community is joined with other communities, some new nodes added or discarded from the community). For the new nodes added to the network, the links of new nodes are checked and linked communities are identified. The local Fire Spread community detection algorithm is executed with new nodes as seed nodes. Detected community is compared with the already exiting communities to decide membership.

For nodes which have deleted from the network, a new threshold, node_threshold is defined which is set to 1% for our work. If more than 1% of the nodes are deleted from a community, local Fire Spread community detection algorithm is executed to check if the community is divided to smaller communities or remains the same.

Our strategy minimizes the need for repeated executions of network level community detection and reduces the execution cost. The algorithm is compared with some of the static algorithms at different snapshots and is presented in the Table 6.14.

Data Sets: Two real-world networks, Facebook and Twitter networks are used. The snapshots are taken in a interval of 7days with total of 24 snapshots for each network. The events such as; new links between participant nodes, old links deleted (few in numbers), new participant nodes included in the network (few in number), participants nodes left the network (very few), observed in the network. LFR and Planted partition artificial networks are also used for the experiment. The networks are modified to work

```
FSA_Dynamic (G, interval_long, interval_short, link_threshold, node_threshold):
Data : G, interval_long, interval_short, link_threshold, node_threshold
Result: Community structure of G
while True do
    timer_long = timer_long + 1
    if timer_long ≥ interval_long then
        Community_structure = FSA(G)
        timer_short = 0
    end
end
for each community in community_structure do
    if new_link added then
        link_added = link_added.append(new_link)
    end
    if new_node added then
        node_added = node_added.append(new_node)
    end
    if timer_short ≥ interval_short then
        if length(link_added) ≥ link_threshold then
            Rerun local_FSA
            update community_strucrure
        end
        if length(node_added) ≥ node_threshold then
            Rerun local_FSA
            update Community_strucrure
        end
        timer_short = 0
    end
    timer_short = timer_short + 1
end
```
Algorithm 9: Modified FSA for time-variant networks

as time-variant networks. The events occurred on the network are: new edges between nodes, old links deleted, some new nodes participated in the network, and some old nodes cease to be part of the network. 10 snapshots are taken for each artificial network.

The modified FSA is acompared with the static community dtection algorithms using average modularity and conductance values across the snapshots. The FSA algorithm is executed at the network level initially once to find the community structure.

The modified FSA algorithm performed better than the static algorithms across all the real-world and artificial networks, as seen in Table 6.14.

6.8 Chapter Summary

By experimenting with synthetic graphs like Relaxed-caveman and planted partition graphs, it is concluded that a graph with community structure will always have longer average shortest path length between its nodes, compared to a random graph having an equal number of nodes and edges. By experimenting with networks with various community

Chapter 6. *Effect of Varying Community Structure on Network* 127

Table 6.14: Comparison of Algorithms for Dynamic Networks

Networks	Algorithms	Nodes	Links	Snapshot	total Snapshot	Avg Modularity	Avg Conductance
LFR	Proposed	1000	14003	Artificial	10	**0.7123**	**0.1752**
	Multilevel					0.7111	0.1839
	Label Prop					0.6987	0.1873
	Infomap					0.6826	0.2815
	Greedy Mod					0.7107	0.1945
	Walktrap					0.6720	0.2683
Planted partition	Proposed	400	3459	Artificial	10	**0.7211**	**0.2216**
	Multilevel					0.6942	0.2430
	Label Prop					0.5398	0.4159
	Infomap					0.6895	0.2784
	Greedy Mod					0.6578	0.2503
	Walktrap					0.6728	0.2711
'Face Book	Proposed	2888	2981	7days	24	0.7983	**0.0947**
	Multilevel					**0.8038**	0.1279
	Label Prop					0.7802	0.1605
	Infomap					0.7762	0.2154
	Greedy Mod					0.7978	0.1219
	Walktrap					0.6209	0.1889
Twitter	Proposed	23370	32831	7days	24	**0.8802**	**0.0407**
	Multilevel					0.8574	0.0412
	Label Prop					0.7832	0.1923
	Infomap					0.8211	0.1847
	Greedy Mod					0.8566	0.0475
	Walktrap					0.8431	0.1034

structures, it is discovered that graphs with more prominent community structures have longer average shortest path lengths. It is also found that, as the size of each community in a network increases, the average shortest path length also gets an increase. The average shortest path length is also found to be longer for the networks having more number of communities. The above mentioned findings may be beneficial for designing communication networks where one of the central objectives is to reduce the overall path length of the network.

A relationship is formulated between the variance in APL (with respect to a random graph having equal nodes and edges) per average degree to the size of each community so that the average size of communities and the number of communities in a network can be predicted in advance, without employing any community detection algorithm. Also, a relationship between the variance in APL (with respect to random graph) to the ratio between average graph degree and average community degree, is formulated.

An efficient enhancement of the community discovery algorithm is proposed, based on community membership matrix and R-radius neighborhood subgraph. The proposed algorithm is compared with some of the state of the art community detection algorithms to validate the effectiveness of the algorithm. The proposed algorithm is an enhancement over the FSA algorithm since it can automatically decide the value of R for the R-radius neighborhood. The uniqueness of this algorithm is that it can work for local community detection to find the community to which a specific seed node belongs, and it does not need to scan the whole graph. This algorithm can assign a single node to more than one community in the presence of overlapping community structure.

Finally, the original FSA algorithm is modified to work with time-variant networks. By experimenting withe real world network and synthetic network, the proposed technique is found to be efficient and comparable with the results of some of the well known static community identification algorithms.

Chapter 7

CONCLUSION AND FUTURE SCOPE

7.1 Conclusion

Community in social network is identification of cluster of nodes which have higher connectivity inside the cluster comparison to outside. Community has a range of applications, such as, terrorist & criminal group detection, information diffusion control, epidemic control strategy, and recommendation system. Various researchers have suggested the existence of community structure in real-world networks. Though many community detection methods are available, still there is ample opportunity for designing a community detection algorithm with low computational complexity that can handle non-overlapping, overlapping, network level, local level, and time-variant community detection.

Various real-world, simulated, and benchmark networks are used to test seven community discovery techniques. For networks with pre-exiting community membership, recall and precision values are employed. In terms of recall and precision, all seven techniques are adequate for synthetic data sets. Recall values for real-world data are not particularly high. In several circumstances, Label Propagation algorithm yielded relatively low modularity ratings, but Infomap and Multilevel methods performed consistently. Even for tiny networks, the Edge Betweenness and Spinglass algorithms have a long execution time. Only connected networks may be used with these two techniques. The modularity, clustering coefficient, and coverage values of synthetic networks fell as the community structure was gradually destroyed, although conductance values rose. Because performance decreases minimally when community structure decreases, it may be stated that the performance parameter is unaffected by community structure quality.

To discover communities in social networks, a unique, nature-inspired Fire Spread algorithm is developed. The suggested algorithm is based on how fire spreads from a single source. It is demonstrated that if each node in the community is linked to at least one-third of the nodes within the community, a two-radius neighbourhood graph is sufficient to search for a local community around a seed node. Given a seed node, an unique probability-based technique is developed for determining the radius of the community. This is used to automate the establishment of recommended FSA radius values. Moreover, the radius prediction algorithm can be used with any of the exiting community detection algorithms to localize the community detection. The suggested approach may be used on a local level with a specified seed node or on a network level by picking random seed nodes automatically. Even in the presence of shared communities, the suggested algorithm works well. The suggested Fire Spread method can identify multiple-resolution hierarchical community structures by adjusting the threshold value. The FSA does not require that the total number of communities in a network be predetermined. Furthermore, the method can allocate a single node to many communities if the node in question is shared by many communities.

The observed communities, identified using FSA with certain well-known social networks, have high precision and recall values. Even in the presence of shared communities, FSA performs well. The FSA does not require that the total number of communities in a network be predetermined. When the algorithm is run locally with different seed nodes, it is discovered that it is capable of finding similar communities with little variation. In terms of conductance and modularity, the suggested Fire Spread algorithm surpassed some of the well-known methods for community discovery on various synthetic and real-world networks. The LFR benchmark networks are also used to assess the proposed method. FSA is also compared to other local community detection techniques that use networks with specified community structure and are based on $F_{measure}$. FSA's performance is found to be superior for some networks and competitive for all of the networks, evaluated.

Using synthetic networks such as the Relaxed-caveman and planted partition networks, it has been determined that a graph with community structure would always have a longer average shortest path length between its nodes than a random graph with an equal number of nodes and edges. Graphs with more significant community structures have longer average shortest path lengths, according to experiments using networks with diverse community patterns. It's also discovered that as the size of each community in a network grows, so does the average shortest path length. For networks with a larger number of communities, the average shortest path length is likewise observed to be longer. The insights presented above might be useful in the design of communication networks when one of the main goals is to lower the network's total path length. Without using any community detection algorithm, a relationship is established between the variance in average shortest path length (with respect to a random graph with equal nodes and edges) per average degree and the size of each community, allowing the average size of communities and the number of communities in a network to be predicted in advance. In addition,

Chapter 7. *Conclusion and Future Scope* 131

a link is established between the variation in average shortest path length (with regard to random graph) and the ratio of average graph degree to average community degree.

The community membership matrix and R-radius neighbourhood subgraph are added to the FSA algorithm to improve it. To confirm the algorithm's efficiency, it is compared to some of the most well-known community detecting techniques. It can determine the value of R for the R-radius neighbourhood automatically. This approach is distinctive in that it may be used for local community detection to determine which community a given seed node belongs to without having to scan the entire graph. In the existence of overlapping community structures, this technique can allocate a single node to several communities.

Finally, the FSA method is tweaked so that it can function with time-varying networks. The suggested methodology is found to be efficient and comparable to the outcomes of some of the well-known static community discovery techniques after experimenting with real-world and synthetic networks.

7.2 Future scope

Community detection is a component of social network analysis that has a variety of uses, including recommendation systems, information dissemination control, epidemic spreading control, and malevolent group identification. Some of the issues of community detection found during the literature study are addressed in this study. There is, however, still room for development.

- The influence of community on average path length on a network is investigated in depth in this study. However, it is necessary to evaluate the other network characteristics that are impacted.

- Synthetic networks can be used to examine the sensitivity of a larger number of community scoring functions to community structure. For overlapping networks, the scope may be expanded.

- The proposed FSA method is intended for networks that are not weighted. The research might be expanded to include weighted networks.

- Other types of networks might benefit from the probabilistic approach for determining average path length in a random graph.

CPSIA information can be obtained
at www.ICGtesting.com
Printed in the USA
BVHW051414270423
663157BV00016B/745

9 781805 280576